THE ASSOCIATION FOR SCOTTISH LITERARY STUDIES
NUMBER FORTY-THREE

FROM THE LINE

SCOTTISH WAR POETRY
1914–1945

*

THE ASSOCIATION FOR SCOTTISH LITERARY STUDIES

The Association for Scottish Literary Studies aims to promote the study, teaching and writing of Scottish literature, and to further the study of the languages of Scotland.

To these ends, the ASLS publishes works of Scottish literature (of which this volume is an example); literary criticism and in-depth reviews of Scottish books in *Scottish Literary Review*; short articles, features and news in *ScotLit*; and scholarly studies of language in *Scottish Language*. It also publishes *New Writing Scotland*, an annual anthology of new poetry, drama and short fiction, in Scots, English and Gaelic. ASLS has also prepared a range of teaching materials covering Scottish language and literature for use in schools.

All the above publications are available as a single 'package', in return for an annual subscription. Enquiries should be sent to:

ASLS, Scottish Literature, 7 University Gardens, University of Glasgow, Glasgow G12 8QH. Telephone/fax +44 (0)141 330 5309 or visit our website at **www.asls.org.uk**

THE ASSOCIATION FOR SCOTTISH LITERARY STUDIES

FROM THE LINE

SCOTTISH WAR POETRY
1914–1945

Edited by David Goldie
and Roderick Watson

GLASGOW

2014

*

Published in Great Britain, 2014
by The Association for Scottish Literary Studies
Scottish Literature
University of Glasgow
7 University Gardens
Glasgow G12 8QH

ASLS is a registered charity no. SC006535

www.asls.org.uk

ISBN: 978-1-906841-16-4

Introduction and Biographies © David Goldie
and Roderick Watson, 2014

A catalogue record for this book
is available from the British Library.

The Association for Scottish Literary Studies acknowledges
support from Creative Scotland towards
the publication of this book.

Typeset by AFS Image Setters Ltd, Glasgow
Printed and bound by Bell & Bain Ltd, Glasgow

Contents

Introduction

What is 'war poetry'? Homer's *Iliad*, after all, must be one of the greatest war poems of all time. In this case however, we chose to make our selection from writers who had lived through the experience of war, at home or abroad, in the thirty-one years between 1914 and 1945. Most of the poems we have chosen were published during or within a few years of the end of hostilities in each conflict. Memory, pain, and inspiration show no respect for time, however, so it is not surprising that some poems took longer to come to the surface. They, too, have their place. Nevertheless, we especially valued poems that spoke with immediacy and intimacy, over those that wanted to editorialise about the terrible wars that stained the first half of the twentieth century. Having said that, the patriotic enthusiasms and popular rhetoric of the early years of the Great War have their place, too, if only as the context within which to set later and darker, hard-won personal wisdom.

Personal wisdom, or a certain resignation perhaps in the balance between dread and peace of mind, was won at a very high cost, by civilians and military personnel alike. The full story of what it was like to endure these wars may never be told because many of those who survived chose not to speak—or could not speak—of what they saw and suffered, and if the dead are eloquent, they are also silent. Some however could turn to poetry to make sense of what was happening, or as a matter of urgency, to exorcise the memory. There was good humour, satire and irony, too, in these writings, as well as a strong and persistently elegiac strain, when poets reflect on their exile so far from what they knew in more peaceful times, or come to mourn the loss of family, friends and comrades in arms. Some of these poems speak of a trauma never quite left behind or a grief that cannot be wholly forgotten, others speak of the sheer thrill of a few moments of intensity never to be found again.

The historian Fritz Stern called the Great War, 'the first calamity of the twentieth century, the calamity from which all other calamities sprang', and we are privileged to be allowed to gain some insight into the human dimension of these two terrible global conflicts by way of the individual voices selected for this volume. And through them we can bear witness to the courage and sacrifice, the humour and the stoicism, of the voiceless millions who suffered and died on a scale of disruption, confusion and carnage that we today—despite, alas, our still continuing acquaintance with calamity—can scarcely even begin to imagine.

'After such knowledge, what forgiveness', T. S. Eliot wrote for 'Gerontion' in 1920, ending the passage with 'These tears are shaken from the wrath-bearing tree.' Little did he know that so many tears had yet to flow, nor that the tree was to flourish so well in the dark years to come. Yet these voices can still be heard, their compassion, their courage in shameful circumstances, their rage, their honesty, their youth and their sheer decent persistence, make a humane challenge to Eliot's opening question, even if its relevance remains as strong as ever.

I.

What makes the First World War especially calamitous, it has often been suggested, is that it was a war for which so few were prepared: a conflict foisted by careless politicians and incompetent generals on populations that were ignorant of its causes and unsuspecting of its horrors, a calamity that would in four short years sweep away the illusions and the trust in authority inculcated by centuries of tradition. 'Never such innocence', Philip Larkin wrote in 'MCMXIV', featuring the Edwardian sunshine and grinning men in queues to enlist—'as if it were all / An August Bank Holiday lark'. The Roman numerals of the poem's title suggest that such times of faith and unquestioning patriotism are now lost in antiquity: 'Never such innocence again.'

Several notable commentators have, though, challenged this view of the war as a turning point, as the moment in which Edwardian cultural innocence was brutally and irrevocably undeceived and in which the harsher, less forgiving worlds of the 1920s and 30s were forged.[i] The period leading up to the First World War was, in many aspects, quite different to that evoked by Larkin, being characterised as much by the recent controversies over the Liberal reforms, the growing threat to established power posed by organised

labour, the escalating militarisation of the Irish Home Rule
struggle, and the vocal and violent public protests of the
Suffragettes. And, for many commentators, the war was not
the scandalous, irresponsible, and tragic throwing away of
life that would come to be remembered variously through
Wilfred Owen, *Oh! What a Lovely War*, and *Blackadder Goes
Forth*, but rather a necessary sacrifice made willingly under
the leadership of capable and forward-thinking generals.[ii]

Yet, there remains much that rings true in Larkin's
description of an innocent people moving eagerly and trust-
ingly towards a war they would have few means of com-
prehending, some awful historical irony in watching a
population dancing carelessly, ignorantly ever closer to the
edge of an abyss. Many Scottish writers, like most of their
fellow Britons, entered the war with considerable enthu-
siasm. For some, it offered a clean break from the compro-
mises and equivocations of everyday life. Rupert Brooke
famously distilled the thrill of enlistment into an image of
'swimmers into cleanness leaping', characterising the volun-
teering soldier as one who leaves behind him 'the sick
hearts that honour could not move', the 'half-men', and
even 'all the little emptiness of love'. This is the purifying
spirit in which the young Alan Mackintosh entered the war,
exhorting recruits to 'Come and learn / To live and die with
honest men' so that they might 'Live clean or go out quick'.
For others, the war offered an opportunity to remind the
world of Scotland's national pride and strong military tradi-
tion. Popular poets such as MacKenzie MacBride might be
expected, in a poem such as 'Shouther Airms!' to indulge a
Scottish jingoism reminiscent of the music hall ('Only gie's
oor pipes and kilt, / And the deil we'll face!'), but more con-
sidered writers such as Neil Munro and Charles Murray
found themselves also accepting the invitation offered by
the war to engage in a facile martial patriotism: the middle-
aged Munro exhorting the young Scot to 'Come awa, Jock,
and kill your man!' and the exile Murray seeming 'keen to
show baith friend an' foe, / Auld Scotland counts for some-
thing still.'

Such sentiments, and their public expression, need to be
noted in any proper consideration of the war's literature.
Firstly because they offer a reminder of the place poetry
had in popular culture in the First World War. In an era

before radio and television broadcasting, in which the
cinema was in its infancy and had yet to speak its first
words, and before modernism and the academy had pushed
it into the hands of an elite, poetry remained an important
medium of public communication. Its visibility in popular
culture, through newspapers, books, and music-hall recita-
tion made it a significant form of public expression, and
sometimes propaganda. But its ubiquity also meant that it
remained available to many people as the proper medium
through which they might attempt to address more personal
responses to the war. The high volume, and somewhat
dubious quality, of this poetic response was noted by,
among many others, the humorous Glasgow paper *The
Bailie*, which noted in October 1914 that 'everyone appears
to be hammering out verse to the best of his, her, or its
ability' and facetiously offered to assist this process by
providing a recipe for the composition of a typical war
poem.[iii]

The second reason for noting this strand of early-war
popular civilian poetry is to illustrate the background from
which the often less celebratory and more intimate poetry
of combatants and the bereaved developed. The conven-
tional narrative of First World War poetry has it following
a trajectory as the war continues from enthusiasm to dis-
illusionment, from rhetorical jingoism to lyrical bitterness,
with the Battle of the Somme in 1916 providing a key turn-
ing point. But, as this volume illustrates, such a view is at
best partial. There are poets here who clearly opposed the
war from its beginning, either stridently like William
Cameron, or with a grim, mordant humour like Charles
Hamilton Sorley. And there are evidently poets, like R. W.
Campbell, who believed wholeheartedly throughout the
conflict that war brought out the best rather than the worst
in men, or who, like Roderick Watson Kerr, were able to
maintain a significant personal faith and resolution in the
face of the horrors they documented in other parts of their
work.

For all its variety, though, the majority of the First World
War poetry printed here does appear to move, as the war
goes on, from an expansive and sometimes careless general-
ising optimism, to a more carefully measured statement, a
more hesitantly detailed reservation. There is considerable

humour, amounting to much more than the generic cheeriness of propaganda, in the masterfully sly, self-serving monologue of Charles Murray's 'Dockens Afore His Peers' or in the amusingly prolix and digressive Spencer, in Alexander Robertson's 'Spencer loquitur: Moi, j'écoute en riant'. There is the relief of being out of the fighting, expressed exuberantly by Charles Scott-Moncrieff in 'Back in Billets', or lyrically in Robertson's 'Written in Hospital, Provence' and the sonnets of Archibald Allan Bowman's 'Rastatt'. But above all, there is the quality that Wilfred Owen characterised as 'the pity of War'. When Owen was drafting a preface for his war poems at Ripon in 1918, he asserted that the projected book was 'not about heroes', and nor would it be 'about deeds, or lands, nor anything about glory, honour, might, majesty, dominion, or power, except War'. 'The Poetry', as he put it, 'is in the pity.'

Much of the more serious, less obviously public poetry here is not about heroes in a conventional sense: something that Roderick Watson Kerr reminds us of bluntly in his common-sense warning, 'Don't say I'm a hero because I was shot; / A bullet won't make one what one is not.' And nor, after some early-war blustering about Scottish martial pride, is it much about national majesty, dominion, or power. What we find instead is a poetry, whether written by combatants or non-combatants, men or women, that attempts and often succeeds in finding much finer, more intimate gradations to measure and record the human cost of the war and the pity it engendered. There are forms of quiet pride and consolation in national and regional community, from the bucolic nostalgia of Mackintosh's 'Anns an Gleann'san Robh Mi Og' to the pastoral elegies of Violet Jacob, and there are examples of steadfast courage and resolution, whether in the soldier's commitment to stand by his fellow sufferers as in Kerr's 'From the Line', or in his will simply to endure, seen in W. D. Cocker's 'Sonnets in Captivity'.

But there is above all an insistent impulse in the most interesting, most humane poetry of the war to reach out beyond personal experience to consider the predicaments of the suffering and the dead: to empathise, as Cocker does, with bereaved families on both sides of the conflict; to show, like Joseph Lee, the human face of the enemy; to put oneself, as Hamish Mann does, in the position of the battlefield corpse; to offer, as do Lee and Mackintosh, the dead an afterlife by engaging them in post-mortem conversation; or in the end simply to honour them in personal, detailed acts of remembrance, such as those made by Mary Symon and J. B. Salmond.

The Scottish poetry of the First World War may not wholly be a record of lost innocence, but, like the poetry of the other combatant nations, it is significant for what it shows of the means by which poetry began, albeit hesitantly and tentatively, to find ways of articulating appropriate, measured, and sometimes very moving responses to an unprecedented experience. It illustrates a process, to borrow a phrase from another Larkin poem, of becoming less deceived; of learning to deal humanely and more realistically, in both form and theme, with the conceptual challenges and the occasional horrors that would, sadly, become such a salient feature of the years that followed.

II.

'Two wars in a lifetime . . . It seemed unfair. Such a short time since 1918.' Naomi Mitchison's words—in the final chapter of her memoir You May Well Ask—speak for the fate of millions in the first half of the twentieth century. Yet in another sense the few years between 1914 and 1939 mark an almost immeasurable gulf of time and experience. And that gulf was created by the 'war to end all wars'— 'After such knowledge, what forgiveness' indeed. Thus it was Cecil Day Lewis in 'Where are the war poets?' who struck the tone of the second war, with his memorable line about being obliged, in the end, to 'defend the bad against the worse' and G. S. Fraser was not alone in thinking that he and his contemporaries had been 'born too late, in this unlucky age' ('To My Friends').

In fact some of the finest Scottish poets started the conflict as conscientious objectors, like Norman MacCaig and Edwin Morgan. Douglas Young chose the moment to make a protest against Westminster's right to enforce conscription in Scotland, and used the ensuing trial and his imprisonment as a not-so-very-well-judged political platform for

Scottish nationalism. Similarly focused, George Campbell
Hay took to the hills to avoid the call, before acceding to
the pressures of the times, and the inescapable realisation
that Hitler's fascism absolutely had to be resisted. Even so,
Sorley MacLean could still confess in uncompromising
terms that 'My fear and hatred of the Nazis [is] even more
than my hatred of the English Empire. My only hope is that
the British and German Empires will exhaust each other'.[iv]
In those years he was hoping for a Soviet triumph but one
could argue that what he eventually got was an American
one. It may be that war should never be justified, and its
implementation is always abominable, yet the moral
urgency of the second war is hard to escape. MacLean had
agonised about fighting fascism in Spain in the 1930s, but
despite his reservations he did not hesitate to go to war
with the Royal Signal Corps in North Africa where he
was wounded three times, severely so at the battle of El
Alamein.

MacLean was not alone, for there was an extraordinary
clustering of Scottish poets in the North African campaign.
(The three infantry brigades of the 51st Highland Division
played a key part in the victory at El Alamein and the sub-
sequent invasion of Italy.) At different times and in different
places G. S. Fraser, Sorley MacLean, George Campbell
Hay, Hamish Henderson, Robert Garioch Sutherland and
Edwin Morgan all served under Morgan's 'pack of stars
from / zenith to horizon blazing down / on mile on mile of
undulating sand', and some of the finest poems of the
entire conflict came from this unlikely band of mostly
non-commissioned enlisted men. MacLean's powerful sense
of his own ancestry sustained him in battle, although his
poem 'Heroes' can ironise that pride, and for all his hatred
of fascism, MacLean, like Henderson, can find only com-
passion for the enemy dead, sharing a common humanity,
commonly oppressed by powers larger than themselves,
commonly given up to death. Henderson's memorable
masterpiece *Elegies for the Dead in Cyrenaica* found the desert
to be a place of mirages and spectral, existential uncertainty,
where opposing forces came to resemble each other,
exchanging equipment in the ebb and flow of battle, facing
mirror images of themselves in the dust and heat. Moti-
vated by the same compassion, perhaps the finest poem of

'total war' came from George Campbell Hay on sentry duty one night in 1943, who watched the distant inferno that was the allied bombardment of Bizerta, a seaport of vital importance for both the German retreat and the allied invasion of Sicily. His lines speak for the hundreds of thousands of civilian deaths in the course of a truly global conflict, just as his 'Esta Selva Selvaggia' invokes Dante in a virtuoso blend of couplets, tercets and linguistic polyphony to express a uniquely despairing invocation of global suffering and hatred. Written in English of an almost unbearable intensity, this must be one of the great war poems of the age, and the poet's national pride takes a darkly bitter twist when he sings 'The swaying landmines lingering down / between Duntocher and the moon / made Scotland and the world one. / At last we found a civilisation / common to Europe and our nation, / sirens, blast, disintegration.'— Hay's vision of a world at war, with his experiences in the desert and Macedonia, marked him for the rest of his life.

Many poems of the conflict reflect this sense of a world gone mad—what Sydney Goodsir Smith saw as a 'Deevil's Waltz'—or the anguish of G. S. Fraser's 'Rostov' in which heroic conflict, after all the rhetoric and the terrible sacrifice, comes down in the end to fratricide and self-destruction. Edwin Muir's 'The River' casts a timeless but strikingly powerful eye on a landscape of destruction. Nor was this confined to the battle front, for the 1939–1945 conflict was 'total war' with a vengeance, and civilian deaths and civilian suffering more than matched the sacrifices of those in uniform. Michael Hinton's 'The Traveller' speaks eloquently for the refugee experience of the dispossessed and the oppressed who faced a 'final solution' all over Europe. Whether an army is in retreat or advancing to victory, Duncan Shaw's 'Pictures' reflects on the fate of the civilian communities left behind. The stoicism of civilian women is caught in Naomi Mitchison's 'The Farm Woman: 1942', while the immediacy and the daily strain of the home front is caught in 'London Burning', or seen again in the giddy nerve-shattered excitements of 'Siren Night'.

The conscripted rank and file of the second war were an unusually literate army. *Poetry London* produced a 'Poets in Uniform' issue in 1941, and Penguin paperbacks, both fiction and non-fiction, were produced in thousands for the troops, to be passed from hand to hand or stocked in Army Welfare libraries. There was a literary scene in Cairo before the war, with the Salamander Group producing *Personal Landscape: an anthology of exile* in 1945 while the Oasis Group produced a poetry collection from Cairo in 1943 wholly written by servicemen and women, followed by series of anthologies after the war from the Salamander Oasis Trust, which built up an extensive archive of service writing from all theatres of conflict.

There was a lively production of poems and songs about everyday army life, humorous, satirical or downright bawdy, giving welcome relief to the frustration and the days of boredom that are part of soldiering too. With his scholarly interest in the Scottish oral tradition, Hamish Henderson proved skilled in this genre with his 'Pioneer Ballad of Section Three', or the 'Ballad of the Stubby Guns', and most especially the rousing music of 'The 51st Division's Farewell to Sicily'. The boost to morale from such work cannot be underestimated, as with Robert Garioch's 'Kriegy Ballad', although other poems about his POW experience (and the prose memoir *Two Men and a Blanket*) take a more serious note. Jack Gillespie's poems were created for his fellow soldiers on topics that will seem familiar to squaddies of any generation, while J. K. Annand's Scots verses from the North Atlantic conflict dramatically invoke first person experience, along with exhaustion, unrelenting cold, and the terror of immediate action.

Sydney Tremayne's 'Elegy', reflects very movingly on the larger perspective—bitter and tragic despite all the fine words—of a conflict that saw over twenty-three million soldiers and nearly thirty-four million civilians killed in over twenty-seven countries across the globe, in a war that truly was a 'world' war. But many of the poems from this conflict—and some of the best—have a smaller and more directly intimate focus. We feel in touch with the immediacy of personal daily experience as Edward Boyd remembers fellow fliers and boyhood friends who lost their lives, or as Colin McIntyre memorialises fallen comrades with a dry wit and challengingly matter-of-fact delivery. There are several such quiet personal elegies in this collection, for if it was 'the people's war' it was always and truly about the people's loss. Nor do the poems miss the lasting trauma of such experience, as a day at the seaside fifteen years after the war throws Robert Garioch back to Libya ('During a Music Festival'); as Alexander Scott wakes with a hammering heart in the night, caught between dreams and memory ('The Twa Images'); or as William Montgomerie remembers his dead brothers even 'Thirty Years After'.

One of the finest poems of the second war was imagined by a non-combatant, born from an anecdote recounted years later in a bar in Aberdeen. Burns Singer's *Transparent Prisoner* tells the story of a soldier captured in the desert war and his experiences as a POW and then as a slave-labourer in a German coalmine. Singer's long poem is an extraordinary act of sympathetic imagination, turning on the moment when the emaciated speaker in the darkness of his imprisonment becomes 'transparent' to himself and the world, just as the bones of a hand can shine through against a flame. Although it does not speak from personal experience, and is too long to be included here, Singer's work must be mentioned, and recommended, as a unique poem that speaks for the suffering of the many thousands of captured and enslaved people in the prisons, factories, mines, death camps and gulags of the war-time and indeed the post-war world.

Theodor Adorno is famous for his often-misinterpreted assertion that to write poetry after Auschwitz is 'barbaric' and 'impossible'. What he was actually drawing attention to was the 'impossibility' of continuing with cultural production in the same vein as the very cultures that produced the objectification of humankind that produced Auschwitz—as if nothing had happened. What is required instead, he argued, is a radical re-thinking of the societies and the ideologies that gave—and continue to give—rise to the objectification of people in the first place. In this respect the passionate distrust of Sorley MacLean and George Campbell Hay—both from an often-despised minority culture and language—may be seen to gain more force. Hay's tears for the Arab population of Bizerta do him honour, and whether such 'objectification' is by way of nuclear attacks on population centres in a policy of mutually assured destruction, or small-scale 'collateral damage' in small-scale skirmishes, or legal assassination by drone strike, we do

well to remember the fate of the nameless, who are still
'paying / the old accustomed tax of common blood.'

In such a context the distrust of those caught up by the
need to defend the bad against the worse may seem more
than just the product of inter-war disillusion. Yet they rose
up when the call came, and destroyed—at terrible cost—the
regime that had embraced the ultimate objectification of
humankind in its plans for a final solution. In such a con-
text these poems, these individual human voices, with their
tales of courage, terror, humour and sacrifice from the
greatest conflict the world has ever seen, still deserve to be
heard.

David Goldie & Roderick Watson

Notes

[i] From George Dangerfield, *The Strange Death of Liberal England*
(London: Constable, 1936) to Charles Emmerson, *1913: The World
before the Great War* (London: Bodley Head, 2013).

[ii] See, for example, Brian Bond, *The Unquiet Western Front: Britain's Role
in Literature and History* (Cambridge: Cambridge University Press,
2002); Gary Sheffield, *Forgotten Victory: The First World War: Myths and
Realities* (London: Review, 2002); Gordon Corrigan, *Mud, Blood and
Poppycock: Britain and the First World War* (London: Cassell, 2004); Dan
Todman, *The Great War: Myth and Memory* (London: Hambledon, 2005).

[iii] 'A War Poem Recipe', *The Bailie*, 14 October 1914, p. 7.

[iv] Letter to Hugh MacDiarmid, 8 March, 1941, quoted by Joy Hendry,
'Sorley MacLean: the Man and his Work', in Raymond J. Ross and
Joy Hendry (eds.), *Sorley MacLean: Critical Essays* (Edinburgh: Scottish
Academic Press, 1986), p. 27.

1914–1918

'A sough o' war gaed through the land
An' stirred it to its benmost heart'

Marion Angus

Remembrance Day

Some one was singing
   Up a twisty stair,
  A fragment of a song,
  One sweet, spring day,
When twelve o'clock was ringing,
  Through the sunny square—

'There was a lad baith frank and free,
Cam' doon the bonnie banks o' Dee
Wi' tartan plaid and buckled shoon,
An' he'll come nae mair to oor toon.'—

'He dwells within a far countree,
Where great ones do him courtesie,
They've gien him a golden croon,
An' he'll come nae mair to oor toon.'—

No one is singing
  Up the twisty stair.
Quiet as a sacrament
  The November day.

Can't you hear it swinging,
   The little ghostly air?—
  Hear it sadly stray
  Through the misty square,
In and out a doorway,
   Up a twisty stair—
Tartan plaid and buckled shoon,
He'll come nae mair to oor toon.

Archibald Allan Bowman

From In the Field

VII

What of our comrades in the forward post?
The fog of war but deepened with the day.
We knew that in that troubled ocean lay
Uncharted shoals, blind rocks, and treacherous coast.
And what of yonder never-ending host
Of wan, unwounded Portuguese? Ah, stay,
Pale sergeant. Do you bleed? You came that way?
What is the tidings? Is the front line lost?
'Nothing is known of posts that lie before
Laventie. At the cross-roads hellish fire
Has cut them off who shouldered the first load.'
Can they live through it? 'They can not retire,
Nor can you reinforce. I know no more
But this. No living thing comes down that road.'

XI

Back from it, back! The quelling mandate rang,
As the mad moment swooped upon the dream.
Straight heathered hillside, mountain, loch, and stream
Flashed out of sight, and but the shrapnel sang,
And greater guns with stunning double clang
Rocked the earth under us. It well might seem
All hell was in the air—not without gleam
Of hope, the worst might prove the final pang.
Men crouched together, shaken as they took
That presence far too massive for their fear,
A quivering sense that something tidal welled
Over their perfect helplessness, and shook
The core of being; yet that being held.
We knew a limber clattered to the rear.

XIII

Grey figures stealing, and a headlong dash
From hedge to house, from house again to hedge,
And fifty rifles levelled on the ledge!
One instant on the aim, and then, the crash!
He went to earth, and vanished in a flash.
And there once more was house, and there was hedge,
With sprouting field, and farm, and ditch with sedge,
And crop-head pollard row and leafless ash—
A cheerless landscape grey, and the profound
Loneliness of the battlefield. The next
Moment trench-mortar shells were on our head;
Another, and the day was sealed and fixed
On front and flank. Among the stricken dead,
One in the skull, behind, his summons found.

From **Rastatt**

III

Within these cages day by day we pace
The bitter shortness of the meted span;
And this and that way variously we plan
Our poor excursions over the poor place,
Cribbed to extinction. Yet remains one grace.
For neither bars nor tented wire can ban
Full many a roving glance that dares to scan
The roomy hill, and wanders into space.
Yea, and remains for ever unrepealed
And unimpaired the free impetuous quest
Of the mind's soaring eye, at length unsealed
To the full measure of a life possessed
Awhile, but never counted, now revealed
Inestimable, wonderful, unguessed.

John Buchan

On Leave

I had auchteen months o' the war,
    Steel and pouther and reek,
Fitsore, weary and wauf,—
    Syne I got hame for a week.

Daft-like I entered the toun,
    I scarcely kenned for my ain.
I sleepit twae days in my bed,
    The third I buried my wean.

The wife sat greetin' at hame,
    While I wandered oot to the hill,
My hert as cauld as a stane,
    But my heid gaun roond like a mill.

I wasna the man I had been,—
    Juist a gangrel dozin' in fits;—
The pin had faun oot o' the warld,
    And I doddered amang the bits.

I clamb to the Lammerlaw
    And sat me doun on the cairn;—
The best o' my freends were deid,
    And noo I had buried my bairn;—

The stink o' the gas in my nose,
    The colour o' bluid in my ee,
And the biddin' o' Hell in my lug
    To curse my Maker and dee.

But up in that gloamin' hour,
    On the heather and thymy sod,
Wi' the sun gaun doun in the Wast
    I made my peace wi' God. . . .

*

I saw a thoosand hills,
   Green and gowd i' the licht,
Roond and backit like sheep,
   Huddle into the nicht.

But I kenned they werena hills,
   But the same as the mounds ye see
Doun by the back o' the line
   Whaur they bury oor lads that dee.

They were juist the same as at Loos
   Whaur we happit Andra and Dave.—
There was naething in life but death,
   And a' the warld was a grave.

A' the hills were graves,
   The graves o' the deid langsyne,
And somewhere oot in the Wast
   Was the grummlin' battle-line.

          *

But up frae the howe o' the glen
   Came the waft o' the simmer een.
The stink gaed oot o' my nose,
   And I sniffed it, caller and clean.

The smell o' the simmer hills,
   Thyme and hinny and heather,
Jeniper, birk and fern,
   Rose in the lown June weather.

It minded me o' auld days,
   When I wandered barefit there,
Guddlin' troot in the burns,
   Howkin' the tod frae his lair.

If a' the hills were graves
   There was peace for the folk aneath
And peace for the folk abune,
   And life in the hert o' death. . . .

          *

Up frae the howe o' the glen
    Cam the murmur o' wells that creep
To swell the heids o' the burns,
    And the kindly voices o' sheep.

And the cry o' a whaup on the wing,
    And a plover seekin' its bield.—
And oot o' my crazy lugs
    Went the din o' the battlefield.

                    *

I flang me doun on my knees
    And I prayed as my hert wad break,
And I got my answer sune,
    For oot o' the nicht God spake.

As a man that wauks frae a stound
    And kens but a single thocht,
Oot o' the wind and the nicht
    I got the peace that I socht.

Loos and the Lammerlaw,
    The battle was feucht in baith,
Death was roon and abune,
    But life in the hert o' death.

A' the warld was a grave,
    But the grass on the graves was green,
And the stanes were bields for hames,
    And the laddies played atween.

Kneelin' aside the cairn
    On the heather and thymy sod,
The place I had kenned as a bairn,
    I made my peace wi' God.

Home Thoughts from Abroad

Aifter the war, says the papers, they'll no be content at hame,
  The lad that hae feucht wi' death twae 'ear i' the mud and
    the rain and the snaw;
For aifter a sodger's life the shop will be unco tame;
  They'll ettle at fortune and freedom in the new lands far awa'.

No me!
By God! No me!
Aince we hae lickit oor faes
And aince I get oot o' this hell,
For the rest o' my leevin' days
I'll mak a pet o' mysel'.
I'll haste me back wi' an eident fit
And settle again in the same auld bit.
And oh! the comfort to snowk again
The reek o' my mither's but-and-ben,
The wee box-bed and the ingle neuk
And the kail-pat hung frae the chimley-heuk!
I'll gang back to the shop like a laddie to play,
Tak doun the shutters at skreigh o' day,
And weigh oot floor wi' a carefu' pride,
And hear the clash o' the countraside.
I'll wear for ordinar' a roond hard hat,
A collar and dicky and black cravat.
If the weather's wat I'll no stir ootbye
Wi'oot an umbrella to keep me dry.
I think I'd better no tak a wife—
I've had a' the adventure I want in life.—
But at nicht, when the door are steeked, I'll sit,
While the bleeze loups high frae the aiken ruit,
And smoke my pipe aside the crook.
And read in some douce auld-farrant book;
Or crack wi' Davie and mix a rummer,
While the auld wife's pow nid-nods in slum'er;
And hark to the winds gaun tearin' bye
And thank the Lord I'm sae warm and dry.

When simmer brings the lang bricht e'en,
I'll daunder doun to the bowling-green,
Or delve my yaird and my roses tend

For the big floo'er-show in the next back-end.
Whiles, when the sun blinks aifter rain,
I'll tak my rod and gang up the glen;
Me and Davie, we ken the püles
Whaur the troot grow great in the howes o' the hills;
And, wanderin' back when the gloamin' fa's
And the midges dance in the hazel shaws,
We'll stop at the yett ayont the hicht
And drink great wauchts o' the scented nicht,
While the hoose lamps kin'le raw by raw
And a yellow star hings ower the law.
Davie will lauch like a wean at a fair
And nip my airm to mak certain shüre
That we're back frae yon place o' dule and dreid,
To oor ain kind warld—

But Davie's deid!
Nae mair gude nor ill can betide him.
We happit him doun by Beaumont toun,
And the half o' my hert's in the mools aside him.

The Great Ones

Ae morn aside the road frae Bray
    I wrocht my squad to mend the track;
A feck o' sodgers passed that way
    And garred me often straucht my back.

By cam a General on a horse,
    A jinglin' lad on either side.
I gie'd my best salute of course,
    Weel pleased to see sic honest pride.

And syne twae Frenchmen in a cawr—
    Yon are the lads to speel the braes;
They speldered me inch-deep wi' glaur
    And verra near ran ower my taes.

And last the pipes, and at their tail
    Oor gaucy lads in martial line.

I stopped my wark and cried them hail,
   And wished them weel for auld lang syne.

*

An auld chap plooin' on the muir
   Ne'er jee'd his heid nor held his han',
But drave his furrow straucht and fair,—
   Thinks I, 'But ye're the biggest man.'

Fisher Jamie

Puir Jamie's killed. A better lad
   Ye wadna find to busk a flee
Or burn a püle or wield a gad
   Frae Berwick to the Clints o' Dee.

And noo he's in a happier land.—
   It's Gospel truith and Gospel law
That Heaven's yett maun open stand
   To folk that for their country fa'.

But Jamie will be ill to mate;
   He lo'ed nae müsic, kenned nae tünes
Except the sang o' Tweed in spate,
   Or Talla loupin' ower its linns.

I sair misdoot that Jamie's heid
   A croun o' gowd will never please;
He liked a kep o' dacent tweed
   Whaur he could stick his casts o' flees.

If Heaven is a' that man can dream
   And a' that honest herts can wish,
It maun provide some muirland stream,
   For Jamie dreamed o' nocht but fish.

And weel I wot he'll up and speir
   In his bit blate and canty way,
Wi' kind Apostles standin' near
   Whae in their time were fishers tae.

He'll offer back his gowden croun
　　And in its place a rod he'll seek,
And bashfu'-like his herp lay doun
　　And speir a leister and a cleek.

For Jims had aye a poachin' whim;
　　He'll sune grow tired, wi' lawfu' flee
Made frae the wings o' cherubim,
　　O' castin' ower the Crystal Sea. . . .

I picter him at gloamin' tide
　　Steekin' the backdoor o' his hame
And hastin' to the waterside
　　To play again the auld auld game;

And syne wi' saumon on his back,
　　Catch't clean against the Heavenly law,
And Heavenly byliffs on his track,
　　Gaun linkin' doun some Heavenly shaw.

R. W. Campbell

The Border Breed

I crave for the style of Kipling, the touch that Tennyson
    made,
To write of the Border gallants who served in a Scots
    Brigade,
Men of the hills and snowdrifts—men of the weaver's
    spool,
Called, and of one ambition, to die like the Border School,
A thousand sons of bold Rievers who dreamed of the
    Battle Yards,
Where bonnets and blades were headed by brave McSteele
    from the Guards.

Proud as the Roman's Caesar—though poor as all hillmen
    are,
Wordless, and strangely silent; communing with things
    that debar
The jest of the snipe from the city; the filth of the things
    unclean—
Now and then wrapt in the raptures of Love and the
    might-have-been,
Mystics, sage dreamers of duty—weird, slow men of the
    hills,
But strong with the fighting passions that yield us the
    battles' thrills.

McSteele was their friend and ruler, a man of that iron
    and blood
Which knits the pride of a regiment, and quenches crime
    in the bud;
A Chief with the fire of the Raiders; one untitled, but
    known
As cream of the folk called gentry—gentry we never
    disown.
And this brave knight of the Borders, with the grace and
    pride of the Guards,
Lived for his bonnets and bayonets; pined for the grim
    Battle Yards.

Time found them dumped near the Narrows, to wrest
  from the Turks the claim
Of Lords of the strip of briny that threatens our Eastern
  fame.
And their job was the job of thrusting—gripping three
  lines of earth
From Enver's dupes and vassals, but vassals of faith and
  worth.
Though shelled by guns that thundered swift death, blood,
  terror, and tears,
The remnant waited for Allah's sake—Allah who bribes
  their fears.

When the song of the guns had ended, McSteele yelled,
  'Charge!' and well
He led them through shrieking shrapnel and a zipping
  Dum-dum Hell.
Men fell, riddled and mangled; the air echoed the weird
  death-shriek,
But on went McSteele, the Guardsman, in a way of which
  regiments speak
Was true of the Guards and Borders,—true of the men
  from the hills,
Who've ever been held for the sortie—the sortie that
  slaughters and kills.

They reached the third of the trenches. Alas! this third
  was a scrape
Of earth that duped air observers, and sent brave
  McSteele to his fate.
So, seeking for their objective, these braves were lured to
  a fire
That staggered, murdered and mangled, and caused the
  order—'Retire!'
From out of a thousand heroes a hundred limped to the
  rear,
Bleeding, battered, and broken—minus the Chief without
  fear.

There's gloom on the hills of the Borders, gloom by the
  shuttle and loom,

For McSteele and his missing gallants—and 'missing' is
    mainly doom.
No praises are printed in papers—no praises are wanted or
    asked,
For Duty's the creed of the Hillmen, Death they expect in
    the task.
*Oh, Britons, thank God for the Borders! Thank God for the men
    who parade,*
*Square-jawed, grim, dour, and determined, in a far-off Lowland
    Brigade!*

The Advice of McPhee

'My advice to you Rookies,' said Private McPhee,
'Is keep your eye down—don't go on the spree,
Don't nod to the Colonel and call him Bill,
Don't ask the S.M. for a fag or a gill,
And, if you want to get on, Salute, Salute,
Salute every ——, Salute, Salute.

'When you're fed up with drill and want a pass,
Arrange that your mother should faint at Mass,
And get your Dad to send on a wire—
"Your mother is dying; please come, McGuire."
You'll *get* your pass—and the loan of a quid
If—your Captain's soft in his heart and "lid."

'Now there's a thing that they calls C.B.
They gives you a dose for being too free
With the Colonel's cook, or a civvy's beer,
Or giving up lip to the Sergeant's dear.
When you gets a few days, just kid you're ill,
Get a sick report and a Number Nine Pill.

'Now, mark my words, you've got to be "fly,"
Dodge drill when you can, but never say die,
When the cook-house goes or the canteen's free
For a pint per man from our P.M.C.,
But remember this—Salute and Salute,
Salute every ——, Salute, Salute.'

The Camerons (K 1)

We're Hielan'men frae Inverness,
    Calcutta, Troon, Mulgy;
We're swanky lads in Hielan' dress,
    Altho' we need some dye
Tae gie oor legs the ghillie touch,
    An' buy some cotton wool
Tae pad oor hose an' show the folks
    We're off the Hielan' school.

CHORUS

We can dress an' chew the Tartan,
An' say Cumarashinchoo;
We can eat twa pun' o' haggis,
Drink a pail o' Hielan' Dew;
We can fecht the Army Polis,
An' pu' the Tug-o'-War;
We're deevils wi' the weemin;
So come, fecht us—if ye daur.

William Cameron

Speak not to me of War!

Speak not to me of sword or gun,
   Of bloody war and strife;
Laud not the inhuman brutes who've won
   And spilt their brother's life.
See yonder bloody corpse-strewn plain,
   Where man has butchered man;
Then write upon your scroll of fame:
   Write 'glorious' if you can!

See yonder lonely woman weep,
   The heart-felt silent tear;
It slowly trickles down her cheek
   For one she loved so dear!
Come, ask the reason of her sigh,
   Why weeps she! What's her care!
She mourns a slaughtered son, that's why
   Show me the glory there!

W. D. Cocker

The Sniper

Two hundred yards away he saw his head;
   He raised his rifle, took quick aim and shot him.
Two hundred yards away the man dropped dead;
With bright exulting eye he turned and said,
   'By Jove, I got him!'
And he was jubilant; had he not won
   The meed of praise his comrades haste to pay?
He smiled; he could not see what he had done;
   The dead man lay two hundred yards away.
He could not see the dead, reproachful eyes,
   The youthful face which Death had not defiled
But had transfigured when he claimed his prize.
   Had he seen this perhaps he had not smiled.
He could not see the woman as she wept
   To hear the news two hundred miles away,
Or through his every dream she would have crept,
   And into all his thoughts by night and day.
Two hundred yards away, and, bending o'er
   A body in a trench, rough men proclaim
Sadly, that Fritz, the merry, is no more.
   (Or shall we call him Jack? *It's all the same.*)

Storm Memories

It is a night of tempest,
  Darkness without a star;
And the wind has assailed the waters,
  And driven them forth to war.
And the twain with a mighty fury
  Beat on the rock-bound coast,
And rank on rank the waves roll on
  Like the charging of a host;
They break beneath the bastion cliffs
  They shatter and are lost.

And here in my lonely dwelling,
  Where the windows quiver and quail,
I sit, and my thoughts are in harmony
  With the booming of the gale.
I sit by the fire and list to the blast,
  Listen and think of the days that are past,
And the guns of Passchendaele.

The tempest comes in gusts;
  It wails through the firs and larches,
It sobs with a dying cadence
  Over the wastes and marches;
It buffets my granite walls
  As though it would test their proof,
It howls its spite in the chimney,
  It rattles the slates on the roof.
And the slanting rain beats down
  And anon comes a volley of hail,
And I think of the bullets that swept the ridge
  On fatal Passchendaele.

The storm abates its frenzy
  And the wind-god draws his breath
And his giant respirations
  Are moans like a man nigh death
And sighs like a sorrowing woman;
  And the rain has ceased to fall,
But it drips with a slow precision
  From the roof and gable-wall.

Drip, drip, drip,
  Now we are counting the losses,
Drip, drip, drip,
  Counting the wooden crosses.
And the wind in the firs and larches
  Takes up the mournful tale.
Drip, drip, drip,
  Lost hopes, lost years,
Drip, drip, drip,
  Blood and tears,
O ridge of Passchendaele!

From **Sonnets in Captivity**

III

Endurance! that's the one outstanding wonder!
What finely tempered steel we mortals are!
What man endures! What trials he goes under
When tested in the crucible of War,
And all the unknown strength and hardihood
Latent within him is made manifest!
We had not guess'd that our frail flesh and blood
Contained the metal to withstand such test.
There is an essence of the spirit when
The soul is strong within us which imparts
To wearied bodies something of its blaze;
Strength lies not then in sinews but in hearts.
Comrades, was it not something in those days
To be a man and to endure with men?

John MacDougall Hay

Their Sons

Thousands of graves of young girls side by side in a
    foreign soil—
Piteous and appalling would be the sight.
So in the exile of death lie the young men far from the
    hills of home and their laughing seas.
The spectacle is tragic and glorious.
Here they have come from the ends of the earth to sleep
    in one battle-soil as in a fold,
With a forest of crosses over their heads.
When from the sea to the mountains the trenches will be
    empty, and the winds will mourn through their
    desolation, the faithful who sleep beneath the crosses
    shall remain, the keepers of the altar of humanity, the
    ransomers guarding Golgotha.
Through summer's heat and winter's frost they, in the
    abandoned battle-fields, shall keep the watch and ward
    which no man sees
Over the new earth which they have purchased with their
    blood.
Naught shall they have of gain or reward but a cross of
    wood,
The supreme symbol of a nation's sacrifice; the bond that
    joins them as brothers to the Son of God.

From **The Call**

Do not think of them as soldiers as they pass by, the
    companions of horses, living among steel and explosives.
They were men like you.
They had their own burdens, anxieties and cares;
A mother to support; children the leaving of whom behind
    was the first death.
To none is home dearer than to those who go forth to
    fight for home.
They left that sanctuary behind.
Never was war more merciless than then; never were they
    braver than in that hour of renunciation.
They, too, had heavy thoughts as they drilled and
    entrenched.
They did not put off humanity when they put on a
    uniform.
They could weep, too.
They also had bad news in letters, and cried at night in
    their dug-out or billet—those devoted lads.
They were not soldiers: they were men,
The best God ever created on this war-scarred earth.
Not as the world calls soldiers.
Military pomp, pride, pageantry and gorgeousness of
    arms—
It moved them not.
Yet as they marched through the City unarmed,
    unpanoplied,
The world could see they were the prophets of their own
    glorious victories—
They, the spirit of a nation issuing incarnate from the
    humble and high doors of the land
To meet the savagery of tall barbaric thrones.

Violet Jacob

To A. H. J.

Past life, past tears, far past the grave,
   The tryst is set for me,
Since, for our all, your all you gave
   On the slopes of Picardy.

On Angus, in the autumn nights,
   The ice-green light shall lie,
Beyond the trees the Northern Lights
   Slant on the belts of sky.

But miles on miles from Scottish soil
   You sleep, past war and scaith,
Your country's freedman, loosed from toil,
   In honour and in faith.

For Angus held you in her spell,
   Her Grampians, faint and blue,
Her ways, the speech you knew so well,
   Were half the world to you.

Yet rest, my son: our souls are those
   Nor time nor death can part,
And lie you proudly, folded close
   To France's deathless heart.

The Field by the Lirk o' the Hill

Daytime an' nicht,
Sun, wind an' rain;
The lang, cauld licht
O' the spring months again.
The yaird's a' weed,
And the fairm's a' still—
Wha'll sow the seed
I' the field by the lirk o' the hill?

Prood maun ye lie,
Prood did ye gang;
Auld, auld am I,
But Oh! life's lang!
Ghaists i' the air,
Whaups cryin' shrill,
An' you nae mair
I' the field by the lirk o' the hill—
Aye, bairn, nae mair, nae mair,
I' the field by the lirk o' the hill!

lirk: *fold*

The Road to Marykirk

To Marykirk ye'll set ye forth,
An' whustle as ye step alang,
An' aye the Grampians i' the North
Are glow'rin' on ye as ye gang.
By Martin's Den, through beech an' birk
A breith comes soughin', sweet and strang,
    Alang the road tae Marykirk.

Frae mony a field ye'll hear the cry
O' teuchits, skirlin' on the wing,
Noo East, noo West, amang the kye,
And smell o' whins the wind'll bring;
Aye, lad, it blaws a thocht to mock
The licht o' day on ilka thing—
For you, that went yon road last spring,
    Are lying deid in Flanders, Jock.

teuchits: *lapwings*

Roderick Watson Kerr

From the Line

Have you seen men come from the Line,
Tottering, doddering, as if bad wine
Had drugged their very souls;
Their garments rent with holes
And caked with mud
And streaked with blood
Of others, or their own;
Haggard, weary-limbed and chilled to the bone,
Trudging aimless, hopeless, on
With listless eyes and faces drawn
Taut with woe?

Have you seen them aimless go
Bowed down with muddy pack
And muddy rifle slung on back,
And soaking overcoat,
Staring on with eyes that note
Nothing but the mire
Quenched of every fire?

Have you seen men when they come
From shell-holes filled with scum
Of mud and blood and flesh,
Where there's nothing fresh
Like grass, or trees, or flowers,
And the numbing year-like hours
Lag on—drag on,
And the hopeless dawn
Brings naught but death, and rain—
The rain a fiend of pain
That scourges without end,
And Death, a smiling friend?

Have you seen men when they come from hell?
If not,—ah, well
Speak not with easy eloquence
That seems like sense

Of 'War and its Necessity'!
And do not rant, I pray,
On 'War's Magnificent Nobility'!

If you've seen men come from the Line
You'll know it's Peace that is divine!
If you've not seen the things I've sung—
Let silence bind your tongue,
But, make all wars to cease,
And work, and work for Everlasting Peace!

The Corpse

It lay on the hill,
A sack on its face,
Collarless,
Stiff and still,
Its two feet bare
And very white;
Its tunic tossed in sight
And not a button there—
Small trace
Of clothes upon its back—
Thank God! it had a sack
Upon its face!

A Dead Man

A dead man dead for weeks
Is sickening food for lover's eye
That seeks and ever seeks
A fair one's beauty ardently!

Did that thing live of late?
That sodden thing of ebony head
With empty holes that gape?
Good God! will I be that, when dead?

Perhaps those blackened bones
Were subtly fashioned hand and wrist
That made sweet violin tones,
Or held a face till lips had kissed!

Perhaps—but, no! it cannot be,
This thing is but a heap of slime—
A hideous mockery—
The man is safe from rotting Time:

Then stick it under ground!
It is a thing for spades not tears;
And make no mourning sound,
And finished, have no fears:

For, glowing in some woman's heart,
He lives embalmed, unchanging, and apart!

Then come! let's kill the memory of this place—
O friends! it had a hideous, ebony face!

Faith

I have leaned on God
And have been comforted by Him:
My fears have been allayed;
My terror of Death has been forgotten;
My frightened heart
Has ceased its knocking;
And my pulse has steadied,
And my resolution cleared and steeled.
I have placed my life in His hands
To take or leave,
To break or fracture—
As a lover gives her all,
Her body and her soul,
Unto the man she loves,
So I have given my all to God,
Surrendered to His Will
In absolute submission:
And in the hour of battle I am unafraid,
And I can put my finger to my nose at Death,
For I am not my own, but God's.

If He should will it,
He will put a bullet thro' my head;
Or tear my limbs asunder with a shell;
Or glean my entrails out;
Or make me foam and choke with gas:
And 'twill be well.

But, if He will it,
He will turn the bullets in their flight;
Will make a stoppage in a gun;
Or make a gunner's hand to tremble,
That his aim be false—

And winds of bullets will cool my cheeks,
And shrapnel fall like blossoms on my head!

Denial

If I should die—chatter only this:—
'A bullet flew by that did not miss!'
I did not give life up because of a friend;
That bullet came thro', and that was the end!

Don't put up a cross where my dung will be laid,
But scatter some wheat—and bread will be made;
Don't say I'm a hero because I was shot;
A bullet won't make one what one is not.

Don't scribble my name upon Honour's scroll
And plaster it up on the Churches hall:
What honour is there in being forced to die?
We slaughter a pig—but we make it a fry!

And what are the odds 'tween the pig and I?
The pig can't help dying—he is forced to die;
And so with myself, when a bullet comes thro'
I simply must die—then why the ado?

Oh! if I should die—chatter only this—
'A bullet flew by that did not miss';
I did not give life up because of a friend;
That bullet came thro'—and *voilà*, the end!'

June, 1918

June! the joyous, sun-filled month of June
When roses, emblems of a heaven, croon
Strange melodies in garden and in hedge
With blithesome birds that sing in emerald edge
Of English lanes; and thousand other flow'rs
As sweet drench incense on the air in show'rs—
Intoxicating wine that gives fair dreams
Of Palaces in Paradise, and streams
Of visions far surpassing Kubla Khan!
When cool sweet winds blow from the woods to fan
Two lovers lying, kissing in the grass
Where sun-lit waters glimpse and, laughing, pass.

June! a writhing, war-gorged month of hell
When steel and iron and high explosive yell
Cursed cacophonies in blasted plains,
With singeing bullets singing in the lanes
Of ripped France; and poisonous vapours drench
With death the air and earth—pocked with trench
And gaping scar—so he who breathes them in
Gulps strangling hands that clutch and tear at him,
And vision sees of no cool Kubla Khan;
When rancid gusts from charnel tree-stumps fan
Two soldiers, clutching, kissing in the grass;
Whose souls leak out in spurting red, and pass!

Joseph Lee

The Bullet

Every bullet has its billet;
   Many bullets more than one:
God! Perhaps I killed a mother
   When I killed a mother's son.

The Green Grass

The dead spake together last night,
   And one to the other said:
   'Why are we dead?'

They turned them face to face about
   In the place where they were laid:
   'Why are we dead?'

'This is the sweet, sweet month o' May,
   And the grass is green o'erhead—
   Why are we dead?

'The grass grows green on the long, long tracks
   That I shall never tread—
   Why are we dead?

'The lamp shines like the glow-worm spark,
   From the bield where I was bred—
   Why am I dead?'

The other spake: 'I've wife and weans,
   Yet I lie in this waesome bed—
   Why am I dead?

'O, I hae wife and weans at hame,
   And they clamour loud for bread—
   Why am I dead?'

Quoth the first: 'I have a sweet, sweet heart,
    And this night we should hae wed—
    Why am I dead?

'And I can see another man
    Will mate her in my stead,
    Now I am dead.'

They turned them back to back about
    In the grave where they were laid:—
    'Why are we dead?'

'I mind o' a field, a foughten field,
    Where the bluid ran routh and red—
    Now I am dead.'

'I mind o' a field, a stricken field,
    And a waeful wound that bled—
    Now I am dead.'

They turned them on their backs again,
    As when their souls had sped,
    And nothing further said.

                    *

The dead spake together last night,
    And each to the other said,
    Why are we dead?

German Prisoners

When first I saw you in the curious street,
Like some platoon of soldier ghosts in grey,
My mad impulse was all to smite and slay,
To spit upon you—tread you 'neath my feet.
But when I saw how each sad soul did greet
My gaze with no sign of defiant frown,
How from tired eyes looked spirits broken down,
How each face showed the pale flag of defeat,
And doubt, despair, and disillusionment,
And how were grievous wounds on many a head,
And on your garb red-faced was other red;
And how you stooped as men whose strength was spent,
I knew that we had suffered each as other,
And could have grasped your hand and cried, 'My
    brother'!

The Carrion Crow

A crow sat on a crooked tree,
And first it cawed, then glowered at me.

Quoth I, 'Thou hoary, hooded crow,
Why do ye glower upon me so?'

'I look upon thee live,' it said,
'That I may better ken thee dead;

'That I may claim thee for my ain
When ye are smoored among the slain.'

The crow perched on that crooked tree,
Nor raised its evil eye frae me.

It perched upon that crooked thorn,
And gazed on me as if in scorn:

'I'll whet my bill upon thy blade
Where thou art lying in the glade;

'I'll pike out baith thy bonnie e'en;
I'll pike the flesh frae off each bane;

'Thy lips that kissed a lover fair,
Got wot! but I will kiss them bare!'

The crow perched on that crooked tree,
Nor raised its evil eye frae me.

'Thou horrid, hooded, hoary crow,
Why do ye glower upon me so?'

'I look upon thee live,' it said,
'That I may better ken thee dead.'

Walter Lyon

I tracked a dead man down a trench

I tracked a dead man down a trench,
  I knew not he was dead.
They told me he had gone that way,
  And there his foot-marks led.

The trench was long and close and curved,
  It seemed without an end;
And as I threaded each new bay
  I thought to see my friend.

I went there stooping to the ground.
  For, should I raise my head,
Death watched to spring; and how should then
  A dead man find the dead?

At last I saw his back. He crouched
  As still as still could be,
And when I called his name aloud
  He did not answer me.

The floor-way of the trench was wet
  Where he was crouching dead:
The water of the pool was brown,
  And round him it was red.

I stole up softly where he stayed
  With head hung down all slack,
And on his shoulders laid my hands
  And drew him gently back.

And then, as I had guessed, I saw
  His head, and how the crown—
I saw then why he crouched so still,
  And why his head hung down.

The Blue is Bright

The blue is bright, the sun
    Is warm to-day.
But both, ere day be done,
    Will fade away.

Thick clouds will be uprolled,
    Black streams of rain
Flood down, and gloom and cold
    Bear sway again.

Fair heaven's a fickle thing,
    Like her own moon;
Though Summer follows Spring,
    Comes Winter soon.

Grief haunts life's festival,
    Makes poor joy shiver:
'Life's years are few in all,
    Death lasts for ever.'

MacKenzie MacBride

Shouther Airms!

We frae Lawlan' toons and fairms:
    And for field whaur lav'rocks wing,
    For the braes whaur burnies sing,
We will shouther airms.

We the Border laddies stoot,
    Frae whaur rang the clash of steel
    And fires flashed frae crag and peel,
When oor clans cam' oot.

Hielan' lads we are wha ask
    That you spare oor Gaelic tongue,
    And oor hames the glens among,
And we'll dae the task!

All together—
    Kissens all o' 'Tamson's' race,
        Only gie's a Scottish lilt,
        Only gie's oor pipes and kilt,
    And the deil we'll face!

Dòmhnall Ruadh Chorùna (Donald MacDonald)

Òran Arras

'Illean, *march at ease!*
    Rìgh na Sìth bhith mar rinn
A' dol chun na strì
    'S chun na cill aig Arras;
'Illean, *march at ease!*

Tha nochd oidhche Luain
    Teannadh suas ri faire,
A' dol chun na h-uaigh
    Far nach fhuasg'lear barrall;
'Illean, *march at ease!*

Tillidh cuid dhinn slàn,
    Cuid fo chràdh lann fala,
'S mar a tha e 'n dàn,
    Roinn le bàs a dh'fhanas;
'Illean, *march at ease!*

Gus ar tìr a dhìon,
    Eadar liath is leanabh,
Mar dhaoin' às an rian
    Nì sinn sgian a tharraing;
'Illean, *march at ease!*

'S lìonmhor fear is tè
    Tha 'n tìr nan geug 'nan caithris,
Feitheamh ris an sgeul
    Bhios aig a' chlèir ri aithris;
'Illean, *march at ease!*

Gura lìonmhor sùil
    Shileas dlùth 's nach caidil
Nuair thig fios on Chrùn
    Nach bi dùil rim balaich;
'Illean, *march at ease!*

The Song of Arras
translated by Ronald Black

Lads, *march at ease!*
   The King of Peace be with us
Going to the strife
   And to the tomb at Arras;
Lads, *march at ease!*

Tonight, Monday night,
   Moving up to guard,
Going to the grave
   Where no bootlace is untied;
Lads, *march at ease!*

Some of us will return unscathed,
   Some in agony of bloody blade,
And, according to our fate,
   Some in the company of death will stay;
Lads, *march at ease!*

To defend our land,
   From grey hairs to child,
Like men gone mad
   We will draw the knife;
Lads, *march at ease!*

Many men and women
   Lie awake in heroes' land
Waiting for the news
   That the clerk has to tell;
Lads, *march at ease!*

Many an eye will weep
   Profusely without sleep
When word comes from the Crown
   That their lads won't be expected;
Lads, *march at ease!*

Patrick MacGill

After Loos
(*Café Pierre le Blanc, Nouex les Mines, Michaelmas Eve, 1915.*)

Was it only yesterday
Lusty comrades marched away?
Now they're covered up with clay.

Seven glasses used to be
Called for six good mates and me—
Now we only call for three.

Little crosses neat and white,
Looking lonely every night,
Tell of comrades killed in fight.

Hearty fellows they have been,
And no more will they be seen
Drinking wine in Nouex les Mines.

Lithe and supple lads were they,
Marching merrily away—
Was it only yesterday?

The Night Before and the Night After the Charge

On sword and gun the shadows reel and riot,
  A lone breeze whispers at the dug-out door,
The trench is silent and the night is quiet,
  And boys in khaki slumber on the floor.
    A sentinel on guard, my watch I keep
    And guard the dug-out where my comrades sleep.

The moon looks down upon a ghost-like figure,
  Delving a furrow in the cold, damp sod.
The grave is ready and the lonely digger
  Leaves the departed to their rest and God.
    I shape a little cross and plant it deep
    To mark the dug-out where my comrades sleep.

A Vision

This is a tale of the trenches
  Told when the shadows creep
Over the bay and traverse
  And poppies fall asleep.

When the men stand still to their rifles,
  And the star-shells riot and flare,
Flung from the sandbag alleys,
  Into the ghostly air.

They see in the growing grasses
  That rise from the beaten zone
Their poor unforgotten comrades
  Wasting in skin and bone,

And the grass creeps silently o'er them
  Where comrade and foe are blent
In God's own peaceful churchyard
  When the fire of their might is spent.

But the men who stand to their rifles
　　See all the dead on the plain
Rise at the hour of midnight
　　To fight their battles again.

Each to his place in the combat,
　　All to the parts they played
With bayonet, brisk to its purpose,
　　Rifle and hand grenade.

Shadow races with shadow,
　　Steel comes quick on steel,
Swords that are deadly silent
　　And shadows that do not feel.

And shades recoil and recover
　　And fade away as they fall
In the space between the trenches,
　　And the watchers see it all.

Pittendrigh MacGillivray

A Woman in the Street
Edina, 1915

O bonnie lad wi' the kilt sae braw
   An' tossel't sporran swingin'—
Wi' dirk at the hip, an' ribbons rid;
   Ye set my hert a-singin'.

What are ye like that's brave an' fine!—
   The Muir-cock or the Eagle?
Your bonnet sets just like a comb,
   Your pride is like the deevil!

Och! sair I grudge ye to the trenches, lad:
   Few flesh an' bane are like ye;
Your knees are hard, your e'en are clean—
   For *you* I'd fecht—God strike me!

Ye wanton rogue! but I love your swing,
   An' weel I guess your fettle!
For a swatch o' you I'd face *my* bit—
   Proud to beget sic metal.

But there he goes: wi' never a glance:
   To that damned hell in Flanders.
My gift is nocht—his seed gangs waste—
   Curse on the cause that squanders!

Squanders the wealth o' Scotland's kind,
   In their high day and flower,
While we wha hae the grace to save
   Stand Kirk-denied Love's dower.

E. A. Mackintosh

Anns an Gleann'san Robh Mi Og

In the Glen where I was young
Blue-bell stems stood close together,
In the evenings dew-drops hung
Clear as glass above the heather.
I'd be sitting on a stone,
Legs above the water swung,
I a laddie all alone,
In the glen where I was young.

Well, the glen is empty now,
And far am I from them that love me,
Water to my knees below,
Shrapnel in the clouds above me;
Watching till I sometimes see,
Instead of death and fighting men,
The people that were kind to me,
And summer in the little glen.

Hold me close until I die,
Lift me up, it's better so;
If, before I go, I cry,
It isn't I'm afraid to go;
Only sorry for the boy
Sitting there with legs aswung
In my little glen of joy,
In the glen where I was young.

Cha Till MacCruimein
Departure of the 4th Camerons

The pipes in the street were playing bravely,
  The marching lads went by,
With merry hearts and voices singing
  My friends marched out to die;
But I was hearing a lonely pibroch
  Out of an older war,
'Farewell, farewell, farewell, MacCrimmon,
  MacCrimmon comes no more.'

And every lad in his heart was dreaming
  Of honour and wealth to come,
And honour and noble pride were calling
  To the tune of the pipes and drum;
But I was hearing a woman singing
  On dark Dunvegan shore,
'In battle or peace, with wealth or honour,
  MacCrimmon comes no more.'

And there in front of the men were marching,
  With feet that made no mark,
The grey old ghosts of the ancient fighters
  Come back again from the dark;
And in front of them all MacCrimmon piping
  A weary tune and sore,
'On the gathering day, for ever and ever,
  MacCrimmon comes no more.'

In Memoriam
Private D. Sutherland killed in action in the German trench, May 16, 1916,
and the others who died.

So you were David's father,
And he was your only son,
And the new-cut peats are rotting
And the work is left undone,
Because of an old man weeping,
Just an old man in pain,
For David, his son David,
That will not come again.

Oh, the letters he wrote you,
And I can see them still,
Not a word of the fighting
But just the sheep on the hill
And how you should get the crops in
Ere the year got stormier,
And the Bosches have got his body,
And I was his officer.

You were only David's father,
But I had fifty sons
When we went up in the evening
Under the arch of the guns,
And we came back at twilight—
O God! I heard them call
To me for help and pity
That could not help at all.

Oh, never will I forget you,
My men that trusted me,
More my sons that your fathers',
For they could only see
The little helpless babies
And the young men in their pride.
They could not see you dying,
And hold you while you died.

Happy and young and gallant,
They saw their first-born go,
But not the strong limbs broken
And the beautiful men brought low,
The piteous writhing bodies,
The screamed, 'Don't leave me, Sir,'
For they were only your fathers
But I was your officer.

The Volunteer

I took my heart from the fire of love,
    Molten and warm not yet shaped clear,
And tempered it to steel of proof
    Upon the anvil-block of fear.

With steady hammer-strokes I made
    A weapon ready for the fight,
And fashioned like a dagger-blade
    Narrow and pitiless and bright.

Cleanly and tearlessly it slew,
    But as the heavy days went on
The fire that once had warmed it grew
    Duller, and presently was gone.

Oh, innocence and lost desire,
    I strive to kindle you in vain,
Dead embers of a greying fire.
    I cannot melt my heart again.

Recruiting

'Lads, you're wanted, go and help,'
On the railway carriage wall
Stuck the poster, and I thought
Of the hands that penned the call.

Fat civilians wishing they
'Could go out and fight the Hun.'
Can't you see them thanking God
That they're over forty-one?

Girls with feathers, vulgar songs—
Washy verse on England's need—
God—and don't we damned well know
How the message ought to read.

'Lads, you're wanted! over there,'
Shiver in the morning dew,
More poor devils like yourselves
Waiting to be killed by you.

Go and help to swell the names
In the casualty lists.
Help to make a column's stuff
For the blasted journalists.

Help to keep them nice and safe
From the wicked German foe.
Don't let him come over here!
'Lads, you're wanted—out you go.'

                         *

There's a better word than that,
Lads, and can't you hear it come
From a million men that call
You to share their martyrdom.

Leave the harlots still to sing
Comic songs about the Hun,
Leave the fat old men to say
Now *we've* got them on the run.

Better twenty honest years
Than their dull three score and ten.
Lads, you're wanted. Come and learn
To live and die with honest men.

You shall learn what men can do
If you will but pay the price,
Learn the gaiety and strength
In the gallant sacrifice.

Take your risk of life and death
Underneath the open sky.
Live clean or go out quick—
Lads you're wanted. Come and die.

The Dead Men

It was yesterday I heard again
The dead man talk with living men,
And watched the thread of converse go
Among the speakers to and fro,
Woven with merriment and wit
And beauty to embroider it;
And in the middle now and then,
The laughter clear of happy men—
Only to me a charnel scent
Drifted across the argument,
Only to me his fair young head
Was lifeless and untenanted,
And in his quiet even tones,
I heard the sound of naked bones,
And in his empty eyes could see
The man who talked was dead, like me.

Then in the conversation's swim,
I leaned across and spoke to him,
And in his dim and dreary eyes
Read suddenly a strange surprise,
And in the touch of his dank hand,
Knew that he too could understand;

So we two talked, and as we heard
Our friends' applause of each dull word
We felt the slow and mournful winds
Blow through the corpse house of our minds,
And the cool dark of underground.
And all the while they sat around
Weighing each listless thing we said,
And did not know that we were dead.

Hamish Mann

The Soldier

'Tis strange to look on a man that is dead
    As he lies in the shell-swept hell,
And to think that the poor black battered corpse
    Once lived like you and was well.

'Tis stranger far when you come to think
    That *you* may be soon like him . . .
And it's Fear that tugs at your trembling soul,
    A Fear that is weird and grim!

The Digger

He was digging, digging, digging, with his little pick and
    spade,
And when the Dawn was rising it was trenches that he
    made;
But when the day was over and the sun was sinking
    red,—
He was digging little Homes of Rest for comrades who
    were dead. . . .

The Barriers

Say, have you ever mused upon Death
    When Death was hovering near?
Each breath you thought was your last sweet breath
    And each sound the last you would hear?

Say, have you ever mused upon Life
    When Death was hovering near,
When all the Earth was athrob with strife
    And the air was shaking with fear?

Then—what were your thoughts in that hour of dread
    When the skeleton passed you by?
Pour forth your tale to the listening Dead,
    Let the night winds echo your sigh.

A Song

Sing me a Song of the Army,
    Of khaki and rifles and drums,
Sing me a ballad of heroes,
    Taking each day as it comes.
Sing of the Colonel who bellows,
    Sing of the Major who swears,
Sing of the slackers who don't care a jot,
    And the Second Lieutenant who cares.
Sing of the raptures of marching
    (I *may* interrupt, but don't grieve!);
But above all come tell me, come tell me
    The glorious myth about leave!

To-day

A rifle fired . . . a groaning man sank down to die . . .
An anguished prayer to his white lips leapt . . .
Far on a highland hill where browsing cattle lie
A waiting woman wept.

Charles Scott-Moncrieff

Back in Billets

We're in billets again, and to-night, if you please,
I shall strap myself up in a Wolsely valise.
What's that, boy? Your boots give you infinite pain?
You can chuck them away: we're in billets again.

We're in billets again now and, barring alarms,
There'll be no occasion for standing to arms,
And you'll find if you'd many night-watches to keep
That the hour before daylight's the best hour for sleep.

We're feasting on chocolate, cake, currant buns,
To a faint German-band obbligato of guns,
For I've noticed, wherever the regiment may go,
That we always end up pretty close to the foe.

But we're safe out of reach of trench mortars and snipers
Five inches south-west of the 'Esses' in Ypres;
—Old Bob, who knows better, pronounces it Yper
But don't argue the point now—you'll waken the sleeper.

Our host brings us beer up, our thirst for to quench,
So we'll drink him good fortune in English and French:
—Bob, who finds my Parisian accent a blemish,
Goes one better himself in a torrent of Flemish.

It's a fortnight on Friday since Christopher died,
And John's at Boulogne with a hole in his side,
While poor Harry's got lost, the Lord only knows
    where;—
May the Lord keep them all and ourselves in His care.

. . . Mustn't think we don't mind when a chap gets laid
    out,
They've taken the best of us, never a doubt;
But with life pretty busy and death rather near
We've no time for regret any more than for fear.

. . . Here's a health to our host, Isidore Deschildre,
Himself and his wife and their plentiful childer,
And the brave *aboyeur* who bays our return;
More power to his paws when he treads by the churn!

You may speak of the Ritz or the Curzon (Mayfair)
And maintain that they keep you in luxury there:
If you've lain for six weeks on a water-logged plain,
Here's the acme of comfort, in billets again.

Iain Rothach (John Munro)

Ar Tìr

Brat shneachda air mullach nam beann,
currachd ceòtha mar liath-fhalt m'an ceann,
feadain is sruthain mòintich
a' leum 's a' dòrtadh,
's le torman a' sporgail measg garbhlach nan gleann,
a' sporgail air ùrlar nan gleann,
aig còsan 's mu shàilean nam mòr-bheann;
féidh ruadh', fir na cròice,
air sliosaibh fraoich ruadh-dhonn—
si Tìr nan Gaisgeach a th' ann,
Tìr nam Beann, nan Gaisgeach, 's nan Gleann,
si Tìr nan Gaisgeach a th' ann.

Our Land
translated by Ronald Black

Mantle of snow on the tops of the hills,
capped with mist like grey hair on their heads,
moorland burns and streams
leaping and gushing,
and noisily rummaging through the wilds of the glens,
rummaging through the floors of the glens,
tucked in the mountains' crevices and rounding their heels;
red deer, antlered stags,
on russet-brown heathered slopes—
such is the Land of the Heroes,
the Land of the Mountains, the Heroes, the Glens,
such is the Land of the Heroes.

Ar Gaisgich a Thuit sna Blàir

'S iomadh fear àlainn òg sgairteil,
ait-fhaoilt air chinn a bhlàth-chrìdh,
tric le ceum daingeann làidir,
ceum aotrom, glan, sàil-ghlan,
dhìrich bràigh nam beann móra,
chaidh a choinneamh a' bhàis—
tric ga fhaireach' roimh-làimh—
a chaidh suas chum a' bhlàir;
's tha feur glas an-diugh 'fàs
air na dh'fhàg innleachdan nàmh,
innleachdan dhubh-sgrios an nàmh a chòrr dheth.

Ged bha cuid dhiubh, nuair bu bheò iad,
tric nach b' mhìn réidh sinn còmhla,
O! thuit iad air Còmhnard na Strì.
Fhuair sinn sìnt' iad le'm bàs-leòintean
an dust eu-dreach', na bha chòrr dhiubh,
an laighe 'sìneadh mar mheòir-shìnt'—
smèideadh, stiùireadh,
sparradh ùr-oidhirpean oirnne,
strì air n-adhart, strì còmhla,
an taobh a thuit iad dol còmhl' rinn,
null thar Còmhnard na Strì.

Bi am chuideachd geàrr-ùin',
dùin do rosg-sgàilean air d' shùil
'n seòmar ionmhais do smaoin
's caoin sholas òg-mhaidne, ciùin-mhaidne, òg-mhéis
ga lìonadh, a' briseadh tre uinneag a' chùil—
'n àite taighe, tadhal d' anma,
fasgadh cuspairean a' mhùirn,
an sin—tog, taisg dealbh orra
'nan laighe mar thuit san raon,
fairich, cluinn,
'Bi'bh deas gu leum 'n àirde
le'r ceum gaisgeil, neo-sgàthach, dàna,
bi'bh null Còmhnard na Strì,
na lagaichibh, bi'bh làidir,
bi'bh 'nam badaibh is pàighibh,
am féin-mhuinghinn leag gu làr dhaibh,

air adhart, air adhart;
seo an rathad,
cuir a' Bhratach an sàs
daingeann àrd
air Sliabh Glòrmhor Deagh-Sìth!'
An smèideadh, an cainnt rinn,
'n rùn-gnìomh air an tug iad an deò
suas, 'nan càradh
air an àr-làr,
air a ghleidheadh dhuinn beò
mar gun snaidheadh fear seòlt'
cuimhneachain cloiche-gun-phrìs.

Our Heroes who Fell in Battle
translated by Ronald Black

Many a handsome young man full of energy
openly welcoming from the warmth of his heart,
so often with step firm and strong,
step light, fresh and clean-heeled,
who climbed the slope of the high mountains,
who went to face death—
often sensing it beforehand—
who went up to the battlefield;
and green grass grows today
on what enemy engines left,
on what enemy engines of total destruction left over.

Though there were those, when alive,
with whom we often disagreed,
O! they fell on the Battlefield.
We found them lying with their fatal wounds
in formless dust, what was left of them,
lying stretched out like pointing fingers—
beckoning, guiding,
spurring us on to fresh efforts,
pressing forward, pressing together,
the very way where they fell when with us
they crossed the Battlefield.

Stay with me for a moment,
close the lids on your eyes
in the treasure-house of your thoughts
with the soft light of young-morning, calm-morning, June-
      morning
filling, breaking through the back window—
instead of house, penetrating your soul,
enveloping the objects of love,
then—make, store a picture of them
lying as they fell in the field,
feel, hear,
'Be ready to leap up
with your heroic, fearless, brave step,
cross the Battlefield,
don't weaken, be strong,
get at them and pay them back,
deflate their self-confidence,
onward, onward;
this is the way,
plant the standard
firm and high
on the Glorious Hill of Good Peace!'
Their beckoning, their speech to us,
the reflex in which they
expired, fixed
on the battle-floor,
preserved for us alive
as if some sculptor had hewn
marble memorials.

Neil Munro

Hey, Jock, are ye glad ye 'listed?

Hey! Jock, are ye glad ye 'listed?
   O Jock, but ye're far frae hame!
What d'ye think o' the fields o' Flanders?
   Jockey lad, are ye glad ye came?
Wet rigs we wrought in the land o' Lennox,
   When Hielan' hills were smeared wi' snaw;
Deer we chased through the seepin' heather,
   But the glaur o' Flanders dings them a'!

This is no' Fair o' Balloch,
   Sunday claes and a penny reel;
It's no' for dancin' at a bridal
   Willie Lawrie's bagpipes squeal.
Men are to kill in the morn's mornin';
   Here we're back to your daddy's trade;
Naething for't but to cock the bonnet,
   Buckle on graith and kiss the maid.

The Cornal's yonder deid in tartan,
   Sinclair's sheuched in Neuve Eglise;
Slipped awa wi' the sodger's fever,
   Kinder that ony auld man's disease.
Scotland! Scotland! little we're due ye,
   Poor employ and skim-milk board.
But youth's a cream that maun be paid for,
   We got it reamin', so here's the sword!

Come awa, Jock, and cock your bonnet,
   Swing your kilt as best ye can;
Auld Dumbarton's Drums are dirlin',
   Come awa, Jock, and kill your man!
Far's the cry to Leven Water
   Where your fore-folks went to war,
They would swap wi' us to-morrow,
   Even in the Flanders glaur!

Charles Murray

A Sough o' War

The corn was turnin', hairst was near,
   But lang afore the scythes could start
A sough o' war gaed through the land
   An' stirred it to its benmost heart.
Nae ours the blame, but when it came
   We couldna pass the challenge by,
For credit o' our honest name
   There could be but the ae reply.
     An' buirdly men, fae strath an' glen,
      An' shepherds fae the bucht an' hill,
    Will show them a', whate'er befa',
      Auld Scotland counts for something still.

Half-mast the castle banner droops,
   The Laird's lament was played yestreen,
An' mony a widowed cottar wife
   Is greetin' at her shank aleen.
In Freedom's cause, for ane that fa's,
   We'll glean the glens an' send them three
To clip the reivin' eagle's claws,
   An' drook his feathers i' the sea.
     For gallant loons, in brochs an' toons,
      Are leavin' shop an' yard an' mill,
    A' keen to show baith friend an' foe,
      Auld Scotland counts for something still.

The grim, grey fathers, bent wi' years,
   Come stridin' through the muirland mist,
Wi' beardless lads scarce by wi' school
   But eager as the lave to list.
We've fleshed o' yore the braid claymore
   On mony a bloody field afar,
But ne'er did skirlin' pipes afore
   Cry on sae urgently to war.

Gin danger's there, we'll thole our share,
   Gie's but the weapons, we've the will,
Ayont the main, to prove again
   Auld Scotland counts for something still.

hairst: *harvest*   sough: *rumour*
bucht: *sheep-fold*   shank: *knitting*
reivin': *thieving*   lave: *rest*

When will the war be by?

'This year, neist year, sometime, never,'
   A lanely lass, bringing hame the kye,
   Pu's at a floo'er wi' a weary sigh,
An' laich, laich, she is coontin' ever
'This year, neist year, sometime, never,
   When will the war be by?'

'Weel, wounded, missin', deid,'
   Is there nae news o' oor lads ava?
   Are they hale an' fere that are hine awa'?
A lass raxed oot for the list to read—
'Weel, wounded, missin', *deid*';
   An' the war was by for twa.

raxed: *reached*

Dockens Afore his Peers
(*Exemption Tribunal*)

Nae sign o' thow yet. Ay, that's me, John Watt o'
    Dockenhill:
We've had the war throu' han' afore, at markets owre a
    gill.
O ay, I'll sit, birze ben a bit. Hae, Briggie, pass the snuff;
Ye winna hinner lang wi' me, an' speer a lot o' buff,
For I've to see the saiddler yet, an' Watchie, honest stock,
To gar him sen' his prentice up to sort the muckle knock,
Syne cry upo' the banker's wife an' leave some settin' eggs,
An' tell the ferrier o' the quake that's vrang aboot the legs.
It's yafa wedder, Mains, for Mairch, wi' snaw an' frost an'
    win',
The ploos are roustin' i' the fur, an' a' the wark's ahin'.
Ye've grun yersels an' ken the tyauve it is to wirk a ferm,
An' a' the fash we've had wi' fouk gyaun aff afore the term;
We've nane to spare for sojerin', that's nae oor wark ava,
We've rents to pey, an' beasts to feed, an' corn to sell an'
    saw;
Oonless we get the seed in seen, faur will we be for meal?
An' faur will London get the beef they leuk for aye at Yeel?
There's men aneuch in sooters' shops, an' chiels in
    masons' yards,
An' coonter-loupers, sklaters, vrichts, an' quarrymen, an'
    cyaurds,
To fill a reg'ment in a week, withoot gyaun vera far,
Jist shove them in ahin' the pipes, an' tell them that it's
    'War';
For gin aul' Scotland's at the bit, there's naething for 't
    but list.
Some mayna like it vera sair, but never heed, insist.
Bit, feich, I'm haverin' on like this, an' a' I need's a line
To say there's men that maun be left, an' ye've exemptit
    mine.
Fat said ye? Fatna fouk hae I enoo' at Dockenhill?
It's just a wastrie o' your time, to rin them throu', but
    still—
First there's the wife—'Pass her,' ye say. Saul! had she
    been a lass
Ye hadna rappit oot sae quick, young laird, to lat her pass,

That may be hoo ye spak' the streen, fan ye was playin'
   cairds,
But seein' tenants tak' at times their menners fae their
   lairds,
I'll tell ye this, for sense an' thrift, for skeel wi' hens an'
   caur,
Gin ye'd her marrow for a wife, ye woudna be the waur.
Oor maiden's neist, ye've heard o' her, new hame fae
   buirdin' squeel,
Faur she saw mair o' beuks than broth, an' noo she's
   never weel,
But fan she's playin' ben the hoose, there's little wird o'
   dwaams,
For she's the rin o' a' the tunes, strathspeys, an' sangs, an'
   psalms;
O' 'Evan' an' 'Neander' baith, ye seen can hae aneuch,
But 'Hobble Jennie' gars me loup, an' crack my thooms,
   an' hooch.
Weel, syne we hae the kitchie deem, that milks an' mak's
   the maet,
She disna aft haud doon the deese, she's at it ear' an' late,
She cairries seed, an' braks the muck, an' gies a han' to
   hyow,
An' churns, an' bakes, an' synes the so'ens, an' fyles
   there's peats to rowe.
An' fan the maiden's friens cry in, she'll mask a cup o'
   tay,
An' butter scones, an' dicht her face, an' cairry ben the
   tray.
She's big an' brosy, reid and roch, an' swippert as she's
   stoot,
Gie her a kilt instead o' cotts, an' thon's the gran' recruit.
There's Francie syne, oor auldest loon, we pat him on for
   grieve,
An', fegs, we would be in a soss, gin he should up an'
   leave;
He's eident, an' has lots o' can, an' cheery wi' the men,
An' I'm sae muckle oot aboot wi' markets till atten'.
We've twa chaps syne to wirk the horse, as sweir as sweir
   can be,
They fussle better than they ploo, they're aul' an' mairret
   tee,

An' baith hae hooses on the ferm, an' Francie never kens
Foo muckle corn gyangs hame at nicht, to fatten up their
   hens.
The baillie syne, a peer-hoose geet, nae better than a feel,
He slivvers, an' has sic a mant, an' ae clog-fit as weel;
He's barely sense to muck the byre, an' cairry in the scull,
An' park the kye, an' cogue the caur, an' scutter wi' the
   bull.
Weel, that's them a'—I didna hear—the laadie i' the gig?
That's Johnnie, he's a littlan jist, for a' he leuks sae big.
Fy na, he isna twenty yet—ay, weel, he's maybe near 't;
Owre young to lippen wi' a gun, the crater would be
   fear't.
He's hardly throu' his squeelin' yet, an' noo we hae a plan
To lat him simmer i' the toon, an' learn to mizzer lan'.
Fat? Gar him list! Oor laadie list? 'Twould kill his mither,
   that,
To think o' Johnnie in a trench awa' in fat-ye-ca't;
We would hae sic a miss at hame, gin he was hine awa',
We'd raither lat ye clean the toon o' ony ither twa;
Ay, tak the wife, the dother, deem, the baillie wi' the
   mant,
Tak' Francie, an' the mairret men, but John we canna
   want.
Fat does he dee? Ye micht as weel speir fat I dee mysel',
The things he hasna time to dee is easier to tell;
He dells the yard, an' wi' the scythe cuts tansies on the
   brae,
An' fan a ruck gyangs throu' the mull, he's thrang at
   wispin' strae,
He sits aside me at the mart, an' fan a feeder's sell't
Taks doon the wecht, an' leuks the beuk for fat it's worth
   fan fell't;
He helps me to redd up the dask, he taks a han' at loo,
An' sorts the shalt, an' yokes the gig, an' drives me fan
   I'm fou.
Hoot, Mains, hae mind, I'm doon for you some sma' thing
   wi' the bank;
Aul' Larickleys, I saw you throu', an' this is a' my thank;
An' Gutteryloan, that time ye broke, to Dockenhill ye
   cam'—
'Total Exemption.' Thank ye, sirs. Fat say ye till a dram?

thow: *thaw*   birze: *squeeze*   knock: *clock*
ferrier: *farrier*   tyauve: *struggle*   sooters': *cobblers'*
coonter-loupers: *counter-jumpers = shopkeepers*; *tinkers*
caur: *calves*   dwaams: *faints*   deese: *a long wooden settle*
roch: *rough*   swippert: *nimble, quick* cotts: *petticoats*
soss: *mess*   can: *ability*   sweir: *lazy*
fussle: *whistle*   feel: *child*   mant: *stutter*
lippen: *trust*   mizzer: *measure*   dells: *digs*
redd up the dask: *tidy the desk*   shalt: *horses*

Murchadh Moireach (Murdo Murray)

Luach na Saorsa

Stad tamall beag, a pheileir chaoil,
Tha dol gu d' uidhe; ged as faoin
Mo cheist—am beil 'nad shraon
    Ro-ghuileag bàis?
'M beil bith tha beò le anam caoin
    Ro-sgart' o thàmh?

An làmh a stiùir thu air do chùrs',
An robh i 'n dàn do chur air iùil
A dh'fhàgadh dìlleachdain gun chùl
    An taigh a' bhròin,
Is cridhe goirt le osann bhrùit'
    Aig mnaoi gun treòir?

An urras math do chlann nan daoin'
Thu guin a' bhàis le d' rinn bhig chaoil
A chur am broilleach fallain laoich
    San àraich fhuair?
'Na eubha bàis am beil an t-saors'
    O cheartas shuas?

Freagairt

'Nam shraon tha caoin bhith sgart' o thàmh,
'Nam rinn bhig chaoil ro-ghuileag bàis,
'S an làmh a stiùir, bha dhi san dàn
    Deur goirt don truagh;
Ach 's uil' iad ìobairt-saors' on àird—
    Tron Bhàs thig Buaidh.

The Value of Freedom
translated by Ronald Black

Stop a little, slender bullet,
While speeding to your end; though vain
My question—is there in your wail
  The forecry of death?
Is anyone alive with gentle soul
  Pre-parted from rest?

The hand that sent you on your way,
Was it predestined to put you on a course
That would leave unsupported orphans
  In the house of grief,
And a bitter heart with sigh tormented
  In a powerless wife?

Is it good surety for mankind
That your slender tip should fatally pierce
Some warrior's healthy breast
  In the cold battlefield?
With his death-cry does there come freedom
  From judgement above?

Answer

My wail is a keen for being parted from rest,
In my slender tip is forecry of death,
And the guiding hand was predestined to bring
  Bitter tears to the damned;
But they are all freedom's sacrifice from above—
  For through Death comes Triumph.

Alexander Robertson

Written in Hospital, Provence

The tent is opened to the breeze
And 'neath its swinging flaps one sees,
Though not their shadowy foliage dark,
The stems of fir-trees, with their bark
Of grey and red. A road goes by
Beyond a row of stakes, not high,
But sharply pointed, joined with wires.
And overhead I hear the choirs
Of birds that, while they sing, do build;
Even as in ages past a guild
Of masons some fair fane might rear
That so God's glory might appear
More dearly and yet chant the while
They chiselled in some rich-wrought aisle.
And just across the rising way
Are dark green bushes, whose leaves sway;
How cool and fresh and smooth they look!
Adown the road there winds a brook
Of sunlight with no babbling air,
But bridged by shadows here and there.
Ah, pleasant shade and pleasant green
And brook for one whose eyes have seen
The power of cruel seas of light
And vast unshadowed deserts white.

*

Sometimes the peasant folk will pass;
Perhaps a strong Provençal lass,
With ruddy face and merry tongue
And o'er her arm a basket slung;
Or women old in donkey cart
With vegetables for the mart;
And turbaned Hindoo soldiers march
With stately gait beneath the arch
Of trees; and, sometimes, up or down
Pass officers with stars or crown;
And horses, straining, on the road;

The great grey motor with its load,—
A small space for the eye to see,
Yet Nature and Humanity.

Spencer loquitur: Moi, j'écoute en riant

'Ah, Robertson, my hour is drawing nigh:
At this, as at all partings, let us sigh,
(As soldiers we can hardly drop a tear,
Unless assured that no one else is near!)
Whither go I? I know not nor can feel
Much interest in the question: 'tis your weal
I ponder o'er. Now listen—did they call?
No! my mistake: I thought I heard the bawl
Of rude commandment—hark to me, old boy:
My powers of reasoning I shall employ
To do you kindness. Regard me; I have been
For ten long years a soldier and between
Yourself and me (the French say, *entre nous*:
And, by the way for hairs they say *cheveux*,
Chevaux for horses, so you must beware
When you are thronéd in the barber's chair)—
What was I saying? Ah, I was about
To tell a story that must not come out:
Long since I wearied of the life of camps
Though true, of course, to him who on our stamps
Proclaims his kingship. And I am most fain
Before I go—perchance to join the slain,
Alas!—to bid you when this war hath end
Break with a life which, as I must contend,
Is, as the Bard of Avon would have said,
"Unprofitable, flat," and where the bread
Of life is spread not with the jam of—well,
I scarce know how to finish; can you tell,
Suggest a fitting finish to my "trope"?'
'What of "the Bard of Avon"? he, I hope
Might haply help us.' 'Ah, but bless you, lad,
I spoke of Shakespeare! even in Petrograd
The guttersnipes can quote him;— the peasants too
Upon the farms that labour:— Surely you

Have not received,— but I must sure return
To my "large utterance," for still I burn
To aid:— ah, there's indeed the shout
Imperious that we may never flout.
Farewell, adieu, adieu, farewell, and ah!
Be heedful of my—how they shout! Ta-ta!!'

J. B. Salmond

Pilgrimage
Being the thoughts of an ex-soldier at Ypres, 8 August 1928

Me, an' Jean, an' the bairn;
The wee lad spierin' an' starin';
Daunderin' quiet an' douce-like doun
The Menin road into Ypres toun.
'Did ye kill ony Germans here?'
Man, it's sair what a laddie'll spier.
An' Jean whispers 'Wheest!'—an' there comes
The band wi' its trumpets an' drums.
There's a glower i' the wee laddie's e'e.
Ay, he's ettlin' ti sojer like me.
An' Jean whispers low in her pain:
'Lord, Ye'll no' lat it happen again!'
Syne the Gate whaur the weary feet trod
Like a white kind o' promise fae God.
An' in silence we're spierin' an' starin'
—Me, an' Jean, an' the bairn.

Me an' Jean,
Her wi' a saft warm licht in her een,
Thankfu' that I am come through,
But trimlin' a wee at the mou',
Prood o' the medals I wear—
The same as the Prince stan'in' there;
Her hand grippin' hard in mine here
—Oh Jeannie! Oh Jeannie, my dear!—
An' I ken a' the things she wud say
—An' Geordie was fond o' her tae.
We saw Geordie's bivvy yestreen,
Me' an' Jean.

Me,
Lookin' yont ower the years juist tae see
Yon War like the ploy of a loon;
But a queer kind o' shiver rins doon
My back as the things dribble in
—A hallikit lauch i' the din,

The sangs, an' the mud, an' the claes,
An' my buits, an' yon glint through the haze
O' anither lad's bayonet, an' lichts
Makin' day o' the darkest o' nichts,
An' the drinkin' our tea fae *ae* can.
—Oh Geordie! Oh Geordie, my man!
An'—deil tak' this dust i' my e'e.
Me!

The Unveiling

Out of the mist of yearnings, prides, and shames
We raise our cairn of glorious regret,
And with God's honour now unite the names
Men signed in bloody sweat.

Lest we forget—for we forget so soon
The gifts so much beyond our valuing—
So much of life laid down in life's high noon,
So much of suffering.

This is no day of pride and joy. Not thus
We come; but as poor failing suppliants will,
To ask for help from those who placed for us
The light upon the hill.

So then to God, Who gave them for our weal,
Who saw their Calvary, we hold so cheap,
Let us now pray for power to purely feel,
And help to truly weep

Tears not of sentiment, but from a heart
That knows how great its many failures are.
God help us give in Peace the thousandth part
Of what they gave in War.

Noble and sweet to die for Fatherland—
They have the guerdon God alone can give;
So here God grant us hope to understand
Nobility to live.

Twenty Years Ago
August 1934

There's a thin rain of music comes across the poppied corn,
  Across the poppied corn and the sun-splashed sea,
Crying, 'Who's a-going venturing, a-venturing, a-venturing,
  Who's a-going venturing with all a man can be?'
O, listen, listen, listen, for it's far, far away,
  The dim remembered country where the ghostly pipers
    blow,
Across a world of sorrows to a green blue day
When boyhood went a-soldiering, a-soldiering, a-soldiering,
  When boyhood went a-soldiering, twenty years ago.

> *So off the white starched collar*
>   *And the neat grey suit,*
> *The crease in the trousers*
>   *And the pointed boot,*
> *The rolled umbrella*
>   *And the bowler hat,*
> *Make them in a bundle—*
>   *That's the end of that.*
> *For it's polish for the buttons*
>   *And dubbin for the boots,*
> *And a D. P. rifle*
>   *For the new recruits.*
> *We're learning 'Tipperary'*
>   *And the squad drill hack,*
> *And we're breaking faulty bayonets*
>   *In a straw-filled sack.*
> *We're studying the language*
>   *That the bugles blow*

*

Lad, can it be twenty years, twenty years, twenty years,
  Lad, can it be twenty years, twenty years ago?

They made the boy a soldier in the passing of a day,
  And Agamemnon's warriors on the windy plains of
    Troy,
And Caesar's legionaries and the guards of Marshal Ney,
  Ay, even the Crusaders had nothing on the boy;

For he fought in France and Flanders mud, in Macedonian
    sand,
    In Africa's green jungle, and in the Russian snow,
And he marched against Jerusalem, and made the
    Promised Land—
The boy that went a-soldiering, a-soldiering, a-soldiering,
    The boy that went a-soldiering, twenty years ago.

> *With poisoned gas they choke him,*
>   *With shell and shock and flame*
> *The beauty of his body*
>   *They mangle and they maim.*
> *And when it all was over,*
>   *They worship for an hour,*
> *And build him a memorial,*
>   *And bring to him a flower.*
> *And as the years piled higher,*
>   *They dipped a bloody pen*
> *Into a well of filthiness*
>   *And killed the boy again.*
> *They branded him a libertine,*
>   *A coward and a sot.*
> *The wrong things were remembered,*
>   *And the promises forgot.*
> *Yes, round his grave they watched unmoved*
>   *The weeds of horror grow,*
> *The boy they swore they'd ne'er forget*
*Just twenty years ago, just twenty years ago, just twenty years
ago.*

The boy is dead in all of us, and War's an ugly thing,
    And the pacifist is right no doubt, and the service man
        is ex.,
And 'Tipperary' nowadays is no great song to sing,
    And there isn't much romance about shell-shock and
        nervous wrecks.
But still we hear the music across the poppied corn,
    Across a world of sorrow the ghostly pipers blow.
And thank God we went soldiering, a-soldiering, a-
    soldiering
    With that boy that went a-soldiering twenty years ago!

Charles Hamilton Sorley

All the hills and vales along

All the hills and vales along
Earth is bursting into song,
And the singers are the chaps
Who are going to die perhaps.
  O sing, marching men,
  Till the valleys ring again.
  Give your gladness to earth's keeping,
  So be glad, when you are sleeping.

Cast away regret and rue,
Think what you are marching to.
Little live, great pass.
Jesus Christ and Barabbas
Were found the same day.
This died, that went his way.
  So sing with joyful breath,
  For why, you are going to death.
  Teeming earth will surely store
  All the gladness that you pour.

Earth that never doubts nor fears,
Earth that knows of death, not tears,
Earth that bore with joyful ease
Hemlock for Socrates,
Earth that blossomed and was glad
'Neath the cross that Christ had,
Shall rejoice and blossom too
When the bullet reaches you.
  Wherefore, men marching
  On the road to death, sing!
  Pour your gladness on earth's head,
  So be merry, so be dead.

From the hills and valleys earth
Shouts back the sound of mirth,
Tramp of feet and lilt of song
Ringing all the road along.

All the music of their going,
Ringing swinging glad song-throwing,
Earth will echo still, when foot
Lies numb and voice mute.
　　On, marching men, on
　　To the gates of death with song.
　　Sow your gladness for earth's reaping,
　　So you may be glad, though sleeping.
　　Strew your gladness on earth's bed,
　　So be merry, so be dead.

When you see millions of the mouthless dead

When you see millions of the mouthless dead
Across your dreams in pale battalions go,
Say not soft things as other men have said,
That you'll remember. For you need not so.
Give them not praise. For, deaf, how should they know
It is not curses heaped on each gashed head?
Nor tears. Their blind eyes see not your tears flow.
Nor honour. It is easy to be dead.
Say only this, 'They are dead.' Then add thereto,
'Yet many a better one has died before.'
Then, scanning all the o'ercrowded mass, should you
Perceive one face that you loved heretofore,
It is a spook. None wears the face you knew.
Great death has made all his for evermore.

Lost

Across my past imaginings
   Has dropped a blindness silent and slow.
My eye is bent on other things
   Than those it once did see and know.

I may not think on those dear lands
   (O far away and long ago!)
Where the old battered signpost stands
   And silently the four roads go

East, west, south and north,
   And the cold winter winds do blow.
And what the evening will bring forth
   Is not for me nor you to know.

Mary Symon

The Soldiers' Cairn

Gie me a hill wi' the heather on't,
   An' a reid sun drappin' doon,
Or the mists o' the mornin' risin' saft
   Wi' the reek owre a wee grey toon.
Gie me a howe by the lang Glen road,
   For it's there 'mang the whin an' fern
(D'ye mind on't, Will? Are ye hearin', Dod?)
   That we're biggin' the Soldiers' Cairn.

Far awa' is the Flanders land
   Wi' fremmit France atween,
But mony a howe o' them baith the day
   Has a hap o' the Gordon green;
It's them we kent that's lyin' there,
   An' it's nae wi' stane or airn,
But wi' brakin' herts, an' mem'ries sair
   That we're biggin' the Soldiers' Cairn.

Doon, laich doon the Dullan sings—
   An' I ken o' an aul' sauch tree,
Where a wee loon's wahnie's hingin' yet
   That's dead in Picardy;
An' ilka win' fae the Conval's broo
   Bends aye the buss o' ern,
Where aince he futtled a name that noo
   I'll read on the Soldiers' Cairn.

Oh! build it fine an' build it fair,
   Till it leaps to the moorland sky—
More, more than death is symbolled there,
   Than tears or triumphs by.
There's the Dream Divine of a starward way
   Oor laggard feet would learn—
It's a new earth's corner-stone we'd lay
   As we fashion the Soldiers' Cairn.

*

Lads in your plaidies lyin' still,
   In lands we'll never see,
This lanely cairn on a hameland hill
   Is a' that oor love can dee;
An' fine an' braw we'll mak' it a',
   But oh, my Bairn, my Bairn,
It's a cradle's croon that'll aye blaw doon
   To me fae the Soldiers' Cairn.

howe: *hollow*   fremmit: *foreign, strange*
hap: *cover*   airn: *iron*
laich: *low*   sauch: *willow*
wahnie: *fishing rod*   buss o' ern: *bush of alder*
futtled: *whittled*

After Neuve Chapelle

We'd a hefty second horseman fae the braes on
   Deveronside,
An' twa bit College birkies like to burst their breeks wi'
   pride;
There was Lauchin' Tam an' 'Curly' an' the ane we ca'ed
   'the Loon,'
Wi' his sowf an' pech an' fosel, fit to wreck the hale
   platoon.
An' they're a' deid or deein'—I've a gey bit clour mysel'—
But I winner fat they're thinkin' i' the Glen, o' Neuve
   Chapelle.

Man, I wish I'd seen the smiddy the nicht the news cam
   in!
The Bailie's beld head noddin', the Soutar clawin' 's chin,
The country clashes fleein' as the sun gied doon the Lecht.
Till the paper geat comes skirlin': 'The Gordons in a
   Fecht.'
Losh! I think I see them loupin'—'Gi'es 't!' 'Heely, man,
   't'll tear!'
'Faur are they?' 'Read it!' 'Fat is 't?' An' the Bailie smores
   a swear

As he hicks an' mants: 'H'm! Fiech—It's wait—I'll need to
    spell'—
(It's a geylies chancy mou'fu' that Frenchy Neuve
    Chapelle).

Syne they'll read about La Bassée an' the red roofs o'
    Aubers,
An' like kitlins in the kinkhost they'll try Armentières;
An' the Smith'll rax his weskit fae the nail upo' the wa'—
'I'm dootin' that's Will Lowry's lot: I'll gi'e the wife a ca'.
Puir Will! to lye oor Hielan' strath for (Lord!) a Street o'
    Hell,
I'll nae gi'e Jinse his full address, I'll jist say New
    Shapelle.'

O sair o' heart they'll be, I ken 't'll pit them aff their
    brose;
An' the Bellman'll be dichtin' mair than sneeshan-draps fae
    's nose,
As the pumphels fill on Sunday, an' aside the pulpit stair
They'll see the Roll o' Honour, an' the names o' deid men
    there.
But the Parson winna haiver: I can hear the rafters ring:
'They have garnered earth's best glory, who have died for
    Home and King.'
(He's the deil to spout, oor billie!) It's a slogan, nae a
    knell,
That'll soun' in grey Kiltairlie owre the graves at Neuve
    Chapelle.

A slogan! Ay, they're needn't. Gang doon the Glen at
    nicht:
There's twa lang loons o' Muirton's at the fireside warm
    an' ticht.
There's Boggies snarin' myaukens, an' his neiper buskin'
    flees,
An' the Mason's at the dambrod for the Belgian refugees.
They're dancin', singin', fiddlin', an' owre a rim o' sea
We're treadin'—ay, we're treadin'—each man a Calvary.
Oh, glens that gave the Gordons, is't you will give as well
The cohorts of the damned and done that heed nae Neuve
    Chapelle?

God! Will they ever wauken, the loons that sit at hame?
While din-faced Sikhs an' Ghurkas fecht to keep oor
    shores fae shame.
Oor kin fae a' the Seven Seas are tummelin' to the fray,
But there's laggards yet on lown hillsides 'neath skies that
    span the Spey,
On braes where Charlie's banner flew, an' Jean sae kindly
    kissed,
Where the very peweet's yammer is a wistfu' 'Loon, gang
    'list'—
Man, I canna thole the thocht o 't. But when this cursed
    welter's deen,
I widna like to be the man that stan's in slacker's sheen.

My bairns'll never blush for me; my teem sark-sleeve'll tell
I did my bit for hame an' them ae day at Neuve Chapelle.

sowf: *heavy breathing*
fosel: *wheezing*
clashes: *chatter*
skirlin': *yelling*
mants: *stutters*
kitlins: *kittens*
rax: *reach*
dichtin': *wiping*
pumphels: *pews*
myaukens: *hares*
buskin' flees: *dressing flies*
lown: *quiet*
teem: *empty*

pech: *panting*
clour: *hurt*
paper geat: *paperboy*
smores: *smothers*
geylies: *rather*
kinkhost: *whooping-cough*
lye: *leave*
sneeshan: *snuff*
slogan: *war cry*
neiper: *neighbour*
dambrod: *draughtboard*
sheen: *shoes*

A Whiff o' Hame
Written as an Introduction to a Christmas Book sent to the fighting men in 1916

A hansel! Lads in khaki,
   An' you in sailor's blue—
But this time it isn't baccy,
   'Woodbines' or 'Honeydew'.
It's neither grub nor grauvat,
   It's neither sark nor sock,
It's nae the Psalms o' Dauvit,
   Nor 'Stop yer ticklin', Jock.'

It's—weesht'.—A norland river
   Gaun soochin' to the sea;
It's the mists abeen Loch Lomond,
   An' the stars owre Benachie.
It's a lovelilt fae a gloamin',
   When a' the world was kind!
It's a step gaun up the loanin'
   O' frien's you left behind;
It's a hand-clasp fae your kindred,
   It's a word fae hearts aflame
Wi' love an' pride o' you, lads,—
   Ay—it's jist a whiff o' Hame.

You're back the surf at Saros,
   Where the cloud-wrack hides the moon,
You're fittin't 'mong the Pharaohs,
   Or bombin' at Bethune;
You're in weary fremmit places
   That oor tongues can hardly name—
But it's couthy fires, kent faces,
   Wi' this wee whiff o' Hame.

Oor Hame! Ah, lad, oot yonder!
   Fa dreams o' suns that shone
On Britain's young-day splendour,
   On glories past and gone?
The eyes are surely holden,
   Dull, dead, that canna see

That the day that's great and golden
  Is the day that gave us Thee—
To stand by trench and halyard,
  To ache, an' fecht, an' fa',
As ye cry: 'The old Land's worth it—
  Dear God, it's worth it a'!'

grauvat: *scarf*
loanin': *pathway*
fremmit: *foreign, strange*

soochin': *sighing, murmuring*
fittin't: *walking*

1939–1945

'There were our own, there were the others'

J. K. Annand

Atlantic 1941

'What gart ye jine the navy, Jock?'
   My faither was a sodger,
He spak eneuch o Flanders glaur
   To mak me be a dodger.

I lippent on a warm dry bed,
   My baccy and my rum,
A cleanly daith and a watery grave
   Gif Davy Jones soud come.

I little thocht to doss me doun
   In a craft sae sma and frail,
Wi hammock slung ablow a deck
   That leaks like the Grey Mear's Tail.

And little I thocht to be lockit in
   A magazine like a jyle,
Or end my days in the choking clart
   O a sea befylt wi ile.

Action Stations

'A-a-all the starboard watch!'
'Shairly no again!
What's the wather like?'
'Cauld, wi sleet and rain.'

'Lofty. Depth-charge sentry.
Knocker. You're stand-by.
Haggis. On the gun.
Shorty. Make some ky.

. . . Watch is all closed up, sir.'
'Keep a good look-out.
Latest wireless signal
Says Jerry is about.'

. . . 'Echo two-three-five!'
'What's it sound like, Ping?'
'Could be a sub, sor.'
'Good show. Hold the thing.'

. . . 'What's it doing now, Ping?'
'Moving roight a bit.'
'O.K. Action stations.
Subby, press that tit!'

Clatter, clatter, dunt.
Seaboots on the deck.
'Batten down all hatches.'
'Wot the bleeding 'eck?'

'Steady as you go.'
'Ay-ay, sir, she's steady.'
'Charges cleared away,
Depths all set and ready.'

'Instant echoes now, sor.'
'Here we go then, squire.
I'm laying even money.
Depth charges! Stand by! Fire!'

Plop, bang, plop.
No a whisper noo,
Waitin on the WOWF
That'll gie the ship a grue.

'Christ, that was a beezer.
I wonder if we got her.'
'I shouldn't be . . . look you
There's wreckage on the water.'

'Out scrambling nets.
Away sea-boat's crew.
To prove we've had a kill
We'll want a bod or two.'

'Aircraft green two-oh!'
'Blast this bludy swell.'
'Here comes Jerry now.'
'Gie the bastard hell.'

'Strafing 'is own matlows.
Mikes you blooming fink.'
'If that's the way they want it
We'll let the bastards sink.'

Arctic Convoy

Intil the pitmirk nicht we northwart sail
Facin the bleffarts and the gurly seas
That ser' out muckle skaith to mortal men.
Whummlin about like a waukrife feverit bairn
The gude ship snowks the waters o a wave.
Swithers, syne pokes her neb intil the air,
Hings for a wee thing, dinnlin, on the crest,
And clatters in the trouch wi sic a dunt
As gey near rives the platin frae her ribs
And flypes the tripes o unsuspectin man.

Northwart, aye northwart, in the pitmirk nicht.
A nirlin wind comes blawin frae the ice,
Plays dirdum throu the rails and shrouds and riggin,
Ruggin at bodies clawin at the life-lines.
There's sic a rowth o air that neb and lungs
Juist canna cope wi sic a dirlin onding.

Caulder the air becomes, and snell the wind.
The waters, splairgin as she dunts her boo,
Blads in a blatter o hailstanes on the brig
And geals on guns and turrets, masts and spars,
Cleedin the iron and steel wi coat o ice.

Northwart, aye northwart, in the pitmirk nicht.
The nirlin wind has gane, a lowness comes;
The lang slaw swall still minds us o the gale.
Restin aff-watch, a-sweein in our hammocks,
We watch our sleepin messmates' fozy braith
Transmogrify to ice upon the skin
That growes aye thicker on the ship-side plates.

Nae mair we hear the lipper o the water,
Only the dunsh o ice-floes scruntin by;
Floes that in the noon-day gloamin licht
Are lily leafs upon my lochan dubh.
But nae bricht lily-flouer delytes the ee,
Nae divin bird diverts amang the leafs,
Nae sea-bird to convoy us on our gait.
In ilka deid-lown airt smools Davy Jones,
Ice-tangle marline spikes o fingers gleg
To claught the bodies o unwary sailors
And hike them doun to stap intil his kist.
Whiles 'Arctic reek' taks on the orra shapes
O ghaistly ships-o-war athort our gait,
Garrin us rin ram-stam to action stations
Then see them melt awa intil the air.

Owre lang this trauchle lasts throu seas o daith,
Wi ne'er a sign o welcome at the port,
Nae 'Libertymen fall in!' to cheer our herts,
But sullen sentries at the jetty-heid
And leesome-lanesome waitin at our birth.

At length we turn about and sail for hame,
Back throu rouch seas, throu ice and snaw and sleet,
Hirdin the draigelt remnant o our flock
Bieldin them weel frae skaith o enemie.
But southwart noo we airt intil the licht
Leavin the perils o the Arctic nicht.

Edward Boyd

Visibility Zero

All day since dawn,
clammy and grey,
on the hills the mist has sat,
immovable as a bailiff,
and through its thick transparency
loom shapes,
the fighter planes,
taut and impatient, tethered whippets,
and sinister, saurian,
low-bellied to the ground,
the bombers.

And in the crew-room, we,
befurred for death, sit waiting,
fettered to earth by tenuous chains of fog;
cigarette smoke, blue and convolute,
swathing us round with boredom,
thick as the outside mist:
listless we sprawl,
and open books lie round ignored,
white pages fluttered open,
like anxious, forsaken faces;
beside them, the battered pages
of the daily journals,
flung aside in ribaldry.

For we have read, in leaden print,
we are Crusaders,
seen our works described,
vaguely recognising congruency,
as in a fairground mirror,
the freakishness has ever, though remote,
resemblance.

The Press has taken us,
anonymous, despised and mongrel,
and decked us out with lineage;

gushing with genealogy,
the people's mighty voice,
in diapaison full, hath said,
'Arthur and his Knights are now returned
and tread the earth.'

For which we render thanks;
it is not given to every man to see
Sir Lancelot in the gutter sprawled,
fish-mouthed and opaque-eyed with alcohol;
Sir Tristam boasting how he stole
some item from Sir Galahad;
and all the modern band of Lyonesse
retailing fornications in the Mess.

ENSA Concert
*In memory of 2nd Lieut. James Peter
Drowned, Dunkirk, 1940.*

A woman with a tired voice,
and a mouth too red,
is singing;
and we are once again
down on the yellow sands,
watching the gulls plunge,
white noiseless streaks across the blue,
and across the bay,
deep in the heat-haze, the blue hills sleep,
the day war swallowed us up.

The words have no meaning,
and the music is senseless,
but memory ignores futility,
and once again the sand
is filtering through our fingers,
and with it goes our youth,
but this we do not know;
heedless of futurity,
proud of our sun-dark bodies and their strength,
proud of our youth, and fearful of it too,

praying for greatness to meet the moment,
the day war swallowed us up.

Did you remember that golden day,
with the drowning man's ultimate irony,
when the water was bobbing with the heads of men,
and the bombers plunged thicker than the gulls.
Did you remember that golden day,
the day war swallowed us up?

Sergeant-Pilot D. A. Crosbie
Coastal Command
Killed in action 1941

I still remember one night we
talked Berkeleyian philosophy,
you proved conclusively to me
that you and I, we could not be.

So now your dictum I shall keep,
you did not drown in waters deep,
you are not dead, I do not weep.

Norman Cameron

Green, Green is El Aghir

Sprawled on the crates and sacks in the rear of the truck,
I was gummy-mouthed from the sun and the dust of the
    track,
And the two Arab soldiers I'd taken on as hitch-hikers
At a torrid petrol-dump, had been there on their hunkers
Since early morning. I said, in a kind of French
'On m'a dit, qu'il y a une belle source d'eau fraîche,
Plus loin, à El Aghir' . . .

              It was eighty more kilometres
Until round a corner we heard a splashing of waters,
And there, in a green, dark street, was a fountain with two
    faces
Discharging both ways, from full-throated faucets
Into basins, thence into troughs and thence into brooks.
Our negro corporal driver slammed his brakes,
And we yelped and leapt from the truck and went at the
    double
To fill our bidons and bottles and drink and dabble.
Then, swollen with water, we went to an inn for wine.
The Arabs came, too, though their faith might have stood
    between.
'After all,' they said, 'it's a boisson,' without contrition.

Green, green is El Aghir. It has a railway-station,
And the wealth of its soil has borne many another fruit,
A mairie, a school and an elegant Salle de Fêtes.
Such blessings, as I remarked, in effect, to the waiter,
Are added unto them that have plenty of water.

G. S. Fraser

Rostov

That year they fought in the snow
On the enormous plain, the rivulets
Thick with the yellow thaw, and darker, dark
With what at distance might be blood or shadows:
Everything melted, everything numbed, broke,
Every hand was pawing at desolation
And the huge, stupid machine felt a shudder.
It did not matter about all the dead
For what better than death in battle
(The sick voice said in the belly,
'What better than death in battle?')
And the heart had been numbed long ago
Against particular pity (yes, and some,
And some have had their pact against all pity:
'If we ask mercy, let it be counted weakness,
And if we repent, let it be counted strategy!')

But the artillery in its tremendous
Asseveration of another existence
Was like the mask of Lenin, thundering power
From a controlled centre. And lumbering
Came the great new tanks, and always
The artillery kept saying, 'You make
An effort but it exhausts itself,
Everything meets its shock.' And some
Seemed to hear in its thunder, just
The syllables of that strong man, 'They want
A war of extermination, let them have it!'
And there was always blinding and stupefying
The snow, the wet, the shivering soddenness:
And a purpose against one roused that meant death.

So the thing began to stagger, lumbering back,
Reeling under these statements, propositions,
The oratory of the last argument death:
Hammering, hammering, hammering home,
'One man is like another, one strength

Like another strength, and the wicked
Shall not prosper for ever, and the turns
Of history bring the innocent to victory;'
The guns lashing like Churchill's sentences
Or the blows of a whip.
  The terrible strength of Tolstoy,
And Dostoevsky's vision, Lenin's silences,
The great, crude, broad-thewed man with innocent eye
Standing like a queer rock in the path:
And lashing death like lightnings from the heavens.
That year it had rained death like apples,
That year the wicked were strong. But remember
That the time comes when the thing that you strike
Rouses itself, suddenly, very terribly,
And stands staring with a terribly patient look
And says, 'Why do you strike me brother? I am Man.'

A Winter Letter
(*To my sister in London, from Asmara*)

Like an unnourished rose I see you now, and yours the
Pallor of that city of soot and pigeons
Where the leaf is pale, that seems to curl its tendrils
Always around the painted green of iron,
I imagine you pale among the pigeon droppings,
And with your eyelids shadowed like the violets
They sell in bunches from their pavement baskets,
And I imagine you not with your old buxomness
But slim like the young ladies in the advertisements,
With your hair preened in a mode of cockney smartness
And your hands in the pockets of a heavy coat . . .
Do you think wistfully as I do, my darling,
These mornings when your heart is not in that city,
Reluctant stroller to the Board of Trade,
Of our glittering and resourceful north, with its
Terminus smell in the morning of cured herrings
And its crackling autumn suburbs of burned leaves?
Though I write in winter, and now except for the hollies
The trees in our old garden are all bare:
Now as they walk these streets of flashing mica,

They puff white steam from their nostrils, men and horses,
And their iron heels strike out sparks from the frosty
    road!
Now the white mist seeps round the red brick baths by
    the sea-front
And the children are girning at play with blue fingers
For a sea-coal fire and the starch of a Scotch high-tea,
Now with nipped red cheeks, the girls walk the streets
    rapidly,
And the shop-window's holly and tinsel can hardly delay.
I think of the swirl of the taffeta schoolgirls at Christmas,
Remembering Bunny whose skin was like cream upon
    milk,
Remembering Joy with her honey-dark skin and dark
    glances,
Remembering Rosemary's chatter and eloquent eyes,
Ahimé! and sigh because war with its swoop and its terror
That pounces on Europe and lifts up a life like a leaf,
Though its snell wind whirl you into a niche where you're
    cosy
Yet its years eat up youth and the hope of fulfilment of
    youth.

And last night I dreamt I returned and therefore I write,
Last night my train had drawn up at a black London
    station,
And there you were waiting to welcome me, strange but
    the same,
And I shook your gloved hands, kissed your light-
    powdered cheek, and was waiting
To see your new flat, and your books, and your hats, and
    your friends,
When I suddenly woke with a lost lonesome head on my
    pillow,
And black Africa turning beneath me towards her own
    dawn,
And my heart was so sore that this dream should be
    snapped at the prologue
That I send you my soreness, dear heart, for the sake of
    this dream.

S.S. City of Benares
(*Drowned refugee children, 1940*)

The bell that tolls my syllables can tell
An underwater tale, clang how there fell
Suddenly out of a surface shouting world
Into dumb calm doomed children, and there curled
(Currents' sick fingers whispering at their hair)
Round them a coiling clutch, was our despair.
Sea's soft sad pressure, like the sprawl of love,
Darkly spreadeagled, so they could not move,
The wide wet mouth was heavy, they would choke,
Till in that cold confusion pity spoke:
'This is a nightmare and one is asleep.
This is a dream, my brave one, do not weep,
Often may drown in dreams and not be dead:
Such weight is mother leaning on your bed.'

But having thought of this to cheat my pain,
That woe and wonder harrows me again,
Fat clouds seem bulked like whales, while through the
    green
Grave tons of twilight, in a submarine
Solidity of air like sea I move,
Pressure of horror how our hate hurts love.
Deeper than grief can plummet, mercy lies,
But not so deep as trust in children's eyes,
Justice is high in heaven, but more high
Blood of the innocent shall smear the sky—
Or think that red the flame of seraph wings,
See stained-glass heaven, where each darling sings
In God's dark luminous world of green and gold
As lovely as death's waters, but less cold:
Think what you will, but like the crisping leaf
In whipped October, crack your thoughts to grief.
In the drenched valley, whimpering and cold,
The small ghosts flicker, whisper, unconsoled.

Olive Fraser

The Home Fleet

Across my lawn, upon the dawn
The broad-keeled cabbages set sail,
A fleet complete with hearts as sweet
As ever yet for England beat,
The borekail and the kail.

Lo, when my lurching galleons ride
Upon the north wind side by side
Tho' 'Guns and butter' Hitler said
'Guns and cabbages' wakes the dead,
A creaking shanty on the air.
The morning thrush wakes up to stare.

Neath the late stars with masts and spars
That yet will fill my pickle jars
'Express' and 'Harbinger' lean and mutter,
'More Heinkels lying about the gutter
In most unholy disrepair!
Whoever can have put them there?'
And 'Guns and cabbages' wakes the deaf,
'Cabbages for the R. A. F.!'

When to their Plate (no lesser there
Than 'Ajax' or bright 'Exeter'!)
My cabbages' hearts are vanished all
And I, their earthy admiral
Stay useless here, some voice will rise
From these poor stumps of argosies
Till 'Guns and cabbages' still I hear
Victorious upon the year.

Robert Garioch

Property

A man should have no thought for property,
he said, and drank down his pint.
Mirage is found in the Desert and elsewhere.
Later, in Libya (sand & scrub,
the sun two weeks to midsummer)
he carried all his property over the sand:
socks, knife and spoon, a dixie,
toilet kit, the Works of Shakespeare,
blanket, groundsheet, greatcoat,
and a water-bottle holding no more water.
He walked with other scorched men
in the dryness of this littoral waste land,
a raised beach without even sea water
with a much damned escarpment
unchanged throughout a day's truck-bumping
or a lifetime of walking without water,
confirming our worst fears of eternity.
Two men only went on whistling,
skidding on a beat-frequency.
Tenderness to music's dissonances,
and much experience of distress in art
was distressed, this time, in life.
A hot dry wind rose, moving the sand,
the sand-shifting Khamsin, rustling over
the land, whistling through hardy sandy
scrub, where sand-snails' brittle
shells on the sand, things in themselves,
roll for ever. Suffusing the sand in the
air, the sun burned in darkness.
No man now whistled, only the sandy wind.
The greatcoat first, then blanket discarded
and the other property lay absurd on the Desert,
but he kept his water-bottle.
In February, in a cold wet climate,
he has permanent damp in his bones
for lack of that groundsheet.
He has a different notion of the values of things.

Kriegy Ballad

Chorus:
Toorally Oorally addy etc.
Here's hoping we're not here to stay.

Yes, this is the place we were took, sir,
And landed right into the bag,
Right outside the town of Tobruk, sir,
So now for some bloody stalag.

There was plenty of water in Derna,
But that camp was not very well kept,
For either you slept in the piss-hole,
Or pissed in the place where you slept.

And then we went on to Benghazi,
We had plenty of room, what a treat!
But I wish that the guard was a Nazi,
He might find us something to eat.

We sailed on the good ship Revalo,
She carried us over the sea,
You climbed up a forty-foot ladder
Whenever you wanted a pee.

And then we went on to Brindisi
With free melons in fields on the way,
Parades there were quite free and easy,
Except that they went on all day.

In transit-camp at Benevento
We stayed a long time, truth to tell,
It was there that we all got the shivers
And were all bloody lousy as well.

The sun it grew hotter and hotter,
The shit-trench was streaked red and brown,
The stew it was like maiden's water
With gnats piss to wash it all down.

With hunger we're nearly demented,
You can see it at once by our looks,
The only ones really contented
Are the greasy fat bastards of cooks.

And then we went on to Capua,
On hard ground we mostly did snooze,
The bedboards got fewer and fewer
As we smashed them up to make brews.

It was there that we got Red Cross parcels
With bully and packets of tea
Would you swop it for . . .
For want of some brew-wood? Not me!

And now it was late in the Autumn
And our clothes they were only a farce,
For torn K.D.2 shorts with no bottom
Send a helluva draught up your arse.

In Musso's fine box-cars we're riding,
All fitted with wheels that are square,
They park us all night in a siding,
But somehow we bloody get there.

At Musso's show-camp at Vetralla
They gave us beds, blankets and sheets,
They'd even got chains in the shit-house,
But still they had no bloody seats.

We were promised a treat for our Christmas
Of thick pasta-shoota, all hot,
But somehow the cooks got a transfer
And shot out of sight with the lot.

So somewhere they wish us good wishes
That we're not all feeling too queer,
And while they are guzzling our pasta
They wish us a happy New Year.

Kriegy: *German slang for P.O.W.*   K.D.2: *Khaki Drill*

Letter from Italy

From large red bugs, a refugee,
I make my bed beneath the sky,
safe from the crawling enemy
though not secure from nimbler flea.
Late summer darkness comes, and now
I see again the homely Plough
and wonder: do you also see
the seven stars as well as I?
And it is good to find a tie
of seven stars from you to me.
Lying on deck, on friendly seas,
I used to watch, with no delight,
new unsuggestive stars that light
the tedious Antipodes.
Now in a hostile land I lie,
but share with you these ancient high
familiar named divinities.
Perimeters have bounded me,
sad rims of desert and of sea,
the famous one around Tobruk,
and now barbed wire, which way I look,
except above—the Pleiades.

During a Music Festival

Cantie in seaside simmer on the dunes,
I fling awa my dowp of cigarette
whaur bairns hae biggit castles out of sand
and watch the reik rise frae the parapet.

Suddenlike I am back in Libya;
yon's the escarpment, and a bleizan plane,
the wee white speck that feeds the luift wi reik,
dirkins a horror-pictur on my brain.

And aye the reik bleeds frae the warld's rim
as it has duin frae Babylon and Troy,
London, Bonn, Edinbro, time eftir time.
And great Beethoven sang a Hymn to Joy.

Flora Garry

Ambulance Depot, 1942

Christmas Eve. The hour between tea and black-out.
The stove reddens and snores in the gathering dusk.
Five tin helmets hang in a row on the wall,
Their little black pot-bellies gleam in the glow of the fire.
Painted on each is a large white capital A.
The telephone stands dumb on its shelf in the nook.
No 'Air Raid Message' comes through, Purple or Red.
The fading sky is void and cold and still
But for the friendly drone of a homing plane,
And the strident intermittent trumpeting
Of the arrowhead formations of the geese
Winging riverwards to seek the sheltering reeds.
In the gloom of the garage the empty vehicles wait,
While we sit here by the snoring stove, and knit.
We are making a Christmas toy, a communal gift,
A scarlet and yellow duck with a bear's snout.

MacDonald is making the head. She had a son.
But his ship, 'overdue must now be presumed lost'.
She carries on as before, brave and bright-eyed.
What can we say? We give her the easiest chair
And fuss with cups of tea and hand cigarettes.
Easier for everyone if she were less brave.

Roberts is making the body of the duck.
She is old. She comes of gentle-folk,
And speaks with an English voice, and avoids draughts.
But she's good at the job and asks for no concessions.
There was someone, we've been told, in the last war.
He fell, leading his men, at Neuve Chapelle.
She likes being here, though we're not quite her sort.
It's something she can do towards settling an old score.

The wings of the duck are made by Clark and Smith
Whose make-up is protective colouration.
They are young. Each wears a wedding ring.
They live from mail to mail, they crouch by the map
And trace the African coast, spelling out names,
Bizerta, Tunis, Tripoli, Tangier,
Renowned in tales of antique chivalry;
Each word a sharp potential two-edged sword
Striking one day, perhaps, at the heart's core.

Watson is making the two feet of the duck.
Leave's postponed. No Christmas engagement now.
They must wait, a few weeks maybe,
Maybe for all time.
She knits, not lifting her head. Best leave her alone.
Shouldn't the black-out be on? We draw the blinds,
Make up the fire—a shovel of dross will do—
Shut out the darkening night and the eerie gusts
Of wind assaulting the hut's ramshackle roof,
Bearing the season's first thin tentative snow.
'Another cigarette? Have you heard this one?'
We laugh, a little too loud. Then silence lasts
A little too long. A muttered emotional curse!
Let's have the wireless on and get the news.
(The news we've learned to hate, but dare not miss.)
A boy's voice sings, high, clear and cruelly sweet:

As we watched at dead of night
Lo! we saw a wondrous light.
Angels singing peace on earth
Telling of the Saviour's birth.

We are making a Christmas toy, a sort of duck,
A comical duck with the blunt, snub snout of a bear.
We are making a toy for some other woman's child.
No one here has any child of her own.

War: 1939–1945

'Faar's Baabie Jeanie's loon? The aal wife hersel
Stans treeshin hame the milkers at the ley park yett.
Faa caas the mornin cairt an fordals neeps an strae,
Wi waages up an risin an fee'd folk sae ull to get?
Baabie Jeanie's Jockie, faar's he?

An yon swack hashin chiel in Willum Sinclair's shop?
He heeld ye oot o langour, sae joco an kin'ly wi't.
'Noo, lassie' to the grunnies: 'Weel, dearie' to the quines,
He's a want ahin the coonter, Willum's sic a strunge breet.
I miss a news wi yon lad. Faar's he?

An Droggie's clivver dother? She could mak her fadder's
    peels.
Nae hoven wyme or clocher, nae beelin, hack or strain
Bit she could ease; an fin royt nackets tummelt greetin at
    their play
She'd rowe up their bleedit sair bits, sen them duncin
    furth again.
The bairns likit Chrissie. Faar's she?

An Cyaarnadellie's foreman? I' the clear Spring nichts
He trystit wi the banker's deemie up at the market place.
Noo, she's skycin roun the gable-eyn, her leen, i the early
    gloam,
Wi a muckle cwyte aboot her an a graavit ower her face.
Cyaarnadellie's foreman, faar's he?'

*

'Speir at the waarslin tides, the desert saans, the caal
  starlicht.
They ken far.'

treeshin: *calling; enticing*
fordals: *stores*
hashin: *hustling*
languor: *boredom*
quines: *young girls*
droggie: *the chemist*
hoven wyme: *swollen stomach*
beelin: *festering sore*
trystit: *met regularly, 'dated'*
skycin: *scurrying*
cwyte: *coat*
speir: *enquire*

yett: *gate*
swack: *agile*
heeld ye: *held you*
joco: *jovial*
strunge breet: *surly chap*
peels: *pills*
clocher: *cough*
royt nackets: *boisterous children*
deemie: *maid, general servant*
her leen: *alone*
graavit: *scarf*

Jack Gillespie

Gillespie's Leave

Complete with mop and biscuit tin,
In which to put some water in,
The Sergeant Major saw me thus,
And called me over without a fuss.

You're due a leave aren't you Lance Naik,
Seven days at Velden would you like,
It hits me like a Louis Crack,
I nearly have a heart attack.

I murmur out a hearty thanks,
Forget about the water tanks,
And go to tell my desert friend,
And see what 'dust' he has to lend.

Gosh! you're lucky, blokes say to me,
Forget I've none since 43,
In fact to put it in clerical ways
I haven't had one for 1003 days.

Then came the time to pack my kit,
Get my clothes creased up a bit,
And pack away the T.M.G.
No longer any use to me.

I meet the storeman show a grin,
Throw my Deny Bundle in.
Away I go for my F.F.I.,
A prelude to the bye and bye.

I stood there in my birthday suit,
Didn't even wear a boot,
And the M.O. with a curious glance,
Says O.K.—put on your pants.

He knew I'd played the game alright,
Kept all women out of sight,
And never sat upon a seat,
Until I'd seen that all was all-reet.

Soon dressed I walk into the hall,
Where on my ears did chance to fall,
The news that two men would not go,
Until the Orderly Room said so.

Of course they gave the men a name,
All the boys said what a shame
The names omitted were to be,
Pte. Boyd and Lance Naik Me.

I praised the Army system well,
And wished the Orderly Room in hell,
Gave all the up & ups 3 cheers,
And burst into a flood of tears.

Now in the barracks I sit & think,
Of how the First & Eighth did link,
How I missed the leave at Philippeville,
Which eludes me now & ever will.

Naik: *Corporal in the British Indian Army.*
T.M.G.: *Thomson Machine Gun.*
F.F.I.: *Free From Infection.*

Deòrsa Mac Iain Deòrsa (George Campbell Hay)

Bisearta

Chì mi rè geàrd na h-oidhche
dreòs air chrith 'na fhroidhneas thall air fàire,
a' clapail le a sgiathaibh,
a' sgapadh 's a' ciaradh rionnagan na h-àird' ud.

Shaoileadh tu gun cluinnte,
ge cian, o 'bhuillsgein ochanaich no caoineadh,
ràn corraich no gàir fuatha,
comhart chon cuthaich uaith no ulfhairt fhaolchon,
gun ruigeadh drannd an fhòirneirt
on fhùirneis òmair iomall fhèin an t-saoghail.
Ach siud a' dol an leud e
ri oir an speur an tostachd olc is aognaidh.

C'ainm nochd a th' orra,
na sràidean bochda anns an sgeith gach uinneag
a lasraichean 's a deatach,
a sradagan is sgreadail a luchd thuinidh,
is taigh air thaigh ga reubadh
am broinn a chèile am brùchdadh toit' a' tuiteam?
Is cò a-nochd tha 'g atach
am Bàs a theachd gu grad 'nan cainntibh uile,
no a' spàirn measg chlach is shailthean
air bhàinidh a' gairm air cobhair, is nach cluinnear?
Cò a-nochd a phàigheas
seann chìs àbhaisteach na fala cumant?

Uair dearg mar lod na h-àraich,
uair bàn mar ghile thràighte an eagail èitigh,
a' dìreadh 's uair a' teàrnadh,
a' sìneadh le sitheadh àrd 's a' call a mheudachd,
a' fannachadh car aitil
's ag at mar anail dhiabhail air dhèinead,
an t-Olc 'na chridhe 's 'na chuisle,
chì mi 'na bhuillean a' sìoladh 's a' leum e.
Tha 'n dreòs 'na oillt air fàire,
'na fhàinne ròis is òir am bun nan speuran,

a' breugnachadh 's ag àicheadh
le 'shoillse sèimhe àrsaidh àrd nan reultan.

Bizerta
translated by George Campbell Hay

I see during the night guard
a blaze flickering, fringing the skyline over yonder,
beating with its wings
and scattering and dimming the stars of that airt.

You would think that there would be heard
from its midst, though far away, wailing and lamentation,
the roar of rage and the yell of hate,
the barking of frenzied dogs from it or the howling of wolves,
that the snarl of violence would reach
from yon amber furnace the very edge of the world;
but yonder it spreads
along the rim of the sky in evil ghastly silence.

What is their name tonight,
the poor streets where every window spews
its flame and smoke,
its sparks and the screaming of its inmates,
while house upon house is rent
and collapses in a gust of smoke?
And who tonight are beseeching
Death to come quickly in all their tongues,
or are struggling among stones and beams,
crying in frenzy for help, and are not heard?
Who tonight is paying
the old accustomed tax of common blood?

Now red like a battlefield puddle,
now pale like the drained whiteness of foul fear,
climbing and sinking,
reaching and darting up and shrinking in size,
growing faint for a moment
and swelling like the breath of a devil in intensity,
I see Evil as a pulse and a heart

declining and leaping in throbs.
The blaze, a horror on the skyline,
a ring of rose and gold at the foot of the sky,
belies and denies
with its light the ancient high tranquillity of the stars.

Esta Selva Selvaggia / This Savage Wood

Relief exults, nostalgia sighs
at yesterday shot from our skies
in smoke and splinters, speeches, lies.
    Today's no ground to stand upon—
    unstable fiction balanced on
    to-morrow and the day that's gone;
    the hair of midnight, finely drawn
    between last evening and the dawn.

Fearful hope and angry fear
guess at to-morrow, paling there,
one man's foul another's fair.

Yesterday? We saw it die
among the shellbursts in the sky,
and heard the snarling headlines cry,
hyenas of a night of fears,
scarlet with tracer, pale with flares,
under distorted guiding-stars.
    Man, violent against his will,
    tore himself open, looked his fill
    and saw; and he is shuddering still.

                    *

The swaying landmines lingering down
between Duntocher and the moon
made Scotland and the world one.
At last we found a civilisation
common to Europe and our nation,
sirens, blast, disintegration.

The house has buried sister, mother.
Sheer chance—a direct hit. Another
near Bou Arâda buried brother.
None was left, and no one mourned.
The telegram has been returned
undelivered, scrapped and burned.

*

The Bofors got him with his bombs away;
crashed airman, hustled from his burning plane
(*Salopard, voilà ce que tu as fait!*)
stumbles dazed to where his stick has strewn
tiles, splintered glass and plaster blotting blood,
pales, stammers: '*Gesù Cristo!* But they should
have struck across the docks. A puff of wind,
a second early! *That* was by my hand?'

*

The sergeant from the Folgore
sips his wine and chats away:
'*Ostia!* It was bizarre.
At San Vincenzo, in the square
behind the church, we found them there.
Two Fridolins, both some days gone,
near them a girl of twenty-one
shot through the face, two caps, a gun,
two glasses and a demi-john.'

'Poisoned the wine she had, I'd say.
But one as he began to sway
still had strength left to make her pay.'

*

'*Merde!*' says the gendarme '*Ces messieurs indigènes*,
why waste one's time on questioning them, when
science can help. Some electricity
applied to the softer parts, and one will see.'

*

Chopping sticks below the prickly pears;
turban, hook nose, cheeks hollow with his years.
He drew his lips back, said: 'There comes a day
when the *Fransâwi* will be swept away.'
Jabbing the earth he twisted his cleaver round—
'Just as I grind this cleaver in the ground,
kilêb, kelbât—dogs, bitches—where we find them,
—*hakdha, hakdha*—thus, thus will we grind them.'

                              *

The Irno Bridge; Salerno in the sun,
while Capo d'Orso in a bluish haze
watches the cobalt waves against him run.

(You'll find the rest in any guide-book's praise.)
This is the land *par excellence* where you sought
select starred ruins, and the parrot phrase
of guides made wearisome the beauty spot.
This is the hell where barking batteries
heap on the old fresh ruins smoking hot.

Here are your newly made antiquities;
new graves and stumps of riddled gables frown
from Paestum to the Arno's Galleries.

The Irno Bridge; the Spring wind from the town
sifts rubble-dust across—ghost-walking yet,
sharp dust of murdered homes now ten months down.

This father, hunched up on the parapet,
peddles his daughter with sly, beaten eyes;
finding no hirer, begs a cigarette.

And past the Osteria, loud with flies,
trail the *perduta gente* of this world,
'artistic rags' and all. What judge denies
peace to these homeless wisps by warblast whirled?

                              *

Ragged and filthy, six years old,
he stumbles on the kerb, and lies
dead still, as if content to hold
this resting pose and never rise.
Hands reach down and put him back,
swaivering, on uncertain feet.
'*Poverini!* They are so weak.
Where and how are they to eat?'

*

'*Haus kaput—maison finie
kaput—capito?—familie.
Alles ist kaput. Compris?*'

'*Er hat uns belogen*—he told us lies.'
'Who wanted war? The poor man dies
in war. He threw dust in our eyes.'

'Only the great make wars,' they say,
'*I pezzi grossi, gros bonnets,
el-kebâr bass* make war to-day.'

'Halûf! Βουλγαρικό σκυλί!
Cretini 'e merda! Βρωμεροί!
Τα Μακαρόνια! Sale Italie!*'

'*N'âd dîn bâbak—salauds*—dogs!
Jene Scheissherrn!* Wops and Frogs,
they're all the same, myte, like the Wogs

*

'What crime was it we suffered for?'
'They started it. We willed no war.'
Listen to yourselves. Beware.

*

Yesterday? We saw it die,
and yet unburied see it lie
rotting beneath a sultry sky.

Where the east pales bleak and grey,
to-morrow is it, or yesterday?
Ask the old men. Can they say?

Yesterday made them. On its walls
they write its end; and down it falls
in blood and pacts and protocols.

We, having seen our yesterday,
blasted away, explained away,
in darkness, having no to-day,
guess at tomorrow dawning grey,
tighten our packstraps for the way.

Dante, *The Divine Comedy. Inferno*, Canto 1, ll. 4–6.

Ahi quanto a dir qual era è cosa dura
esta selva selvaggia e aspra e forte
che nel pensier rinova la paura!

Ah me! how hard a thing it is to say
What was this forest savage, rough, and stern,
Which in the very thought renews the fear.

Folgore: *an Italian Division reformed to fight the Germans in Italy.*
Ostia!: *By the Host!*
I Fridolin: *Italian nickname for the Germans*
Fransâwi: *Frenchman*
perduta gente: *lost people—see* Inferno *Canto 3.*
Poverini: *poor little things*
I pezzi grossi: *the big knobs*
gros bonnet: *big-wigs*
el-kebâr bass: *only the great*
Halûf!: *Pig!*
Βουλγαρικό σκυλί!: *Bulgarian dog!*
Cretini 'e merda!: *Filthy cretins!*
Βρωμεροὶ!: *Stinkers!*
Τα Μακαρόνια!: *The Macaronis!*
N'âd dîn bâbak: *Curse the faith of your father!*
Salauds: *Bastards*
Jene Scheissherrn!: *Shits, all of them!*

Hamish Henderson

from *Elegies for the Dead in Cyrenaica*

FIRST ELEGY
End of a Campaign

There are many dead in the brutish desert,
    who lie uneasy
among the scrub in this landscape of half-wit
stunted ill-will. For the dead land is insatiate
and necrophilous. The sand is blowing about still.
Many who for various reasons, or because
    of mere unanswerable compulsion, came here
and fought among the clutching gravestones,
    shivered and sweated,
cried out, suffered thirst, were stoically silent, cursed
the spittering machine-guns, were homesick for Europe
and fast embedded in quicksand of Africa
    agonised and died.
And sleep now. Sleep here the sleep of the dust.

There were our own, there were the others.
Their deaths were like their lives, human and animal.
There were no gods and precious few heroes.
What they regretted when they died had nothing to do with
    race and leader, realm indivisible,
laboured Augustan speeches or vague imperial heritage.
(They saw through that guff before the axe fell.)
    Their longing turned to
the lost world glimpsed in the memory of letters:
an evening at the pictures in the friendly dark,
two knowing conspirators smiling and whispering secrets;
    or else
a family gathering in the homely kitchen
with Mum so proud of her boys in uniform:
    their thoughts trembled
between moments of estrangement, and ecstatic moments
of reconciliation: and their desire
crucified itself against the unutterable shadow of someone
whose photo was in their wallets.
Then death made his incision.

There were our own, there were the others.
Therefore, minding the great word of Glencoe's
son, that we should not disfigure ourselves
with villainy of hatred; and seeing that all
have gone down like curs into anonymous silence,
I will bear witness for I knew the others.
Seeing that littoral and interior are alike indifferent
and the birds are drawn again to our welcoming north
why should I not sing them, the dead, the innocent?

SEVENTH ELEGY
Seven Good Germans

*The track running between Mekili and Tmimi was at one time a
kind of no-man's-land. British patrolling was energetic; and there
were numerous brushes with German and Italian elements. El
Eleba lies about half-way along this track.*

     Of the swaddies
  who came to the desert with Rommel
there were few who had heard (or would hear) of El Eleba.
They recce'd,
    or acted as medical orderlies
or patched up their tanks in the camouflaged workshops
and never gave a thought to a place like El Eleba.

To get there, you drive into the blue, take a bearing
and head for damn-all. Then you're there. And where are
   you?

—Still, of some few who did cross our path at El Eleba
there are seven who bide under their standing crosses.

The first a Lieutenant.
   When the medicos passed him
for service overseas, he had jotted in a note-book
to the day and the hour keep me steadfast there is only
the decision and the will

     the rest has no importance

The second a Corporal.
      He had been in the Legion
and had got one more chance to redeem his lost honour.
What he said was
Listen here, I'm fed up with your griping—
if you want extra rations, go get 'em from Tommy!
You're green, that's your trouble. Dodge the column, pass the
    buck
and scrounge all you can—that's our law in the Legion.
You know Tommy's got 'em. . . . He's got mineral waters,
and beer, and fresh fruit in that white crinkly paper
and God knows what all! Well, what's holding you back?
Are you windy or what?
      Christ, you 'old Afrikaners'!
If you're wanting the eats, go and get 'em from Tommy!

The third had been a farm-hand in the March of Silesia
and had come to the desert as fresh fodder for machine
    guns.
His dates are inscribed on the files, and on the cross-piece.

The fourth was a lance-jack.
      He had trusted in Adolf
while working as a chemist in the suburb of Spandau.
His loves were his 'cello, and the woman who had borne
    him
two daughters and a son. He had faith in the Endsieg.
THAT THE NEW REICH MAY LIVE prayed the flyleaf
    of his Bible.

The fifth a mechanic.
      All the honour and glory,
the siege of Tobruk and the conquest of Cairo
meant as much to that Boche as the Synod of Whitby.
Being wise to all this, he had one single headache,
which was, how to get back to his sweetheart (called Ilse).
—He had said
    Can't the Tommy wake up and get weaving?
if he tried, he could put our whole Corps in the bag.
May God damn this Libya and both its palm-trees!

The sixth was a Pole
      —or to you, a Volksdeutscher—
who had put off his nation to serve in the Wehrmacht.
He siegheiled, and talked of 'the dirty Polacken',
and said what he'd do if let loose among Russkis.
His mates thought that, though 'just a polnischer
   Schweinhund',
he was not a bad bloke.
      On the morning concerned
he was driving a truck with mail, petrol and rations.
The M.P. on duty shouted five words of warning.
He nodded
    laughed
      revved
        and drove straight for El Eleba
not having quite got the chap's Styrian lingo.

The seventh a young swaddy.
        Riding cramped in a lorry
to death along the road which winds eastward to Halfaya
he had written three verses in appeal against his sentence
which soften for an hour the anger of Lenin.

   Seven poor bastards
   dead in African deadland
  (tawny tousled hair under the issue blanket)
    wie einst Lili
   dead in African deadland

     einst Lili Marlene

Anzio April

Headlines at home. The gangrel season varies,
And Spring has gained a beach-head with our blood.
I've half a mind to kiss the blooming Jerries
And then just beat it while the going's good.
I'll bed down where deserters live on berries . . .
I'll play at possum in yon cork-oak wood . . .
    Machine-guns prate, but dannert flowers, this Spring.
    Over the grave all creatures dance and sing.

Phil shows the latest snap of his bambino.
The new mail's brought a great big box of tricks
For Donny, lucky bastard,—but for me no
Reminders: not a sausage—naethin—nix!
We hear of 'heavy fighting by Cassino'
But still no sign of jeeps on Highway Six . . .
    In Rome the fascists lie between soft sheets
    And numskull death his little tabor beats.

The watching Jerries sight a convoy's funnels:
It's coming into range now, Anzio-bound.
Their railway gun emerges from a tunnel's
Commodious depth, and plonks a single round
A hundred yards beyond one mucker's gunwales.
I bet they'd feel much safer underground!
    This fight one's better off inside the ring.
    Over the grave all creatures dance and sing.

Last night we got a bash from Fritz's 'arty'
And then his mucking jabos gave us hell.
Our mediums up and joined the mucking party.
At last our mucking planes appeared as well.
Now thirteen Jocks are dead as Bonaparty.
(Yon Heinie in the tank's begun to smell).
    Lilac in bloom: the cold's White Guard retreats
    And numskull death his little tabor beats.

Kenny's bomb-happy: I'm a ruddy poet.
By Christ, my case is worse and that's a fact.
Maybe I'm nuts. Maybe I'll start to show it.
Sometimes I think that all the rest are cracked.
They're on the spot, and hell they hardly know it
. . . Or so you'd think, the damfool way they act.
  Spud's writing home, and Eddie thinks he's Bing.
  Over the grave all creatures dance and sing.

Snap out of that. Brigades of battered swaddies
Have got to stay and shoot—or lose their pants;
While strange to say our Jocks (the muckle cuddies)
Have still an inclination to advance.
Down Dead-end Road, and west among the wadis
They'll pipe and make the Jerries do the dance.
  Next month the race. Today we run the heats,
  And numskull death his little tabor beats.

Red Neil, whom last I saw at lifting tatties
Pulls-through his rifle, whistles *Tulach Gorm.*
. . . Two drops of rain. We know whose warning that is.
A plum-hued cloud presents in proper form
(The old court-holy-water diplomat) his
Most courteous declaration of the storm.
The dance is on. Strike up a Highland fling!
  Over the grave all creatures dance and sing.
  (And numskull death his little tabor beats.)

The 51st Highland Division's Farewell to Sicily

The pipie is dozie, the pipie is fey;
He wullnae come roon' for his vino the day.
The sky ow'r Messina is unco and grey,
   An' a' the bricht chaulmers are eerie.

Then fare weel, ye banks o' Sicily,
Fare ye weel, ye valley and shaw.
There's nae Jock will mourn the kyles o' ye.
   Puir bliddy swaddies are wearie.

Fare weel, ye banks o' Sicily,
Fare ye weel, ye valley and shaw.
There's nae hame can smoor the wiles o' ye.
   Puir bliddy swaddies are wearie.

Then doon the stair and line the waterside,
Wait your turn, the ferry's awa'.
Then doon the stair and line the waterside.
   A' the bricht chaulmers are eerie.

The drummie is polisht, the drummie is braw
He cannae be seen for his webbin' ava.
He's beezed himsel' up for a photy an a'
   Tae leave wi' his Lola, his dearie.

Sae fare weel, ye dives o' Sicily
(Fare ye weel, ye shieling an' ha');
We'll a' mind shebeens and bothies
   Whaur kind signorinas were cheerie.

Fare weel, ye banks o' Sicily
(Fare ye weel, ye shieling an' ha');
We'll a' mind shebeens and bothies
   Whaur Jock made a date wi' his dearie.

Then tune the pipes and drub the tenor drum
(Leave your kit this side o' the wa').
Then tune the pipes and drub the tenor drum.
   A' the bricht chaulmers are eerie.

Pipe tune 'Farewell to the Creeks'

J. F. Hendry

London Before Invasion, 1940

Walls and buildings stand here still, like shells,
Hold them to the ear. There are no echoes even
Of the seas that once were. That tide is out
Beyond the valleys and hills.

Days dawn and die, while the city assumes the distance of
    stars.
It is the absence of the heart
In the ebbing seas of heaven,
An ebbing beyond laughter and too tense for tears.

Now, imagination floats, a weed, on water's vacancy.
Faces of women, lit with conscience, past or future
Of men gone, wear one garland of stone features.
Flowers have a girl's irrelevance, and mind is no
    prescience.

Flood-tides returning may bring with them blood and fire,
Blenching with wet panic spirit that must be rock.
May bring a future tossed and torn, as slippery as wrack.
All time adrift in torrents of war.

Question and Answer

How we could ever have come to this pass?
Is all we are asking. Each of our
Bursts of anti-aircraft fire
Hangs a torn wound of questions in the air.

How we could ever, like cattle at grass,
Drift with shadowless clouds, unaware,
Into this era of lightnings and war?
There is no shelter, now or ever, from that answer.

The Return

Now the soldier has come home.

He has fought his way back
To the faces of the gnome-children
With still magic in their glances.

Wearing the green birk in his hat
And clad in the brown earth
He has torn barbed sorrow down
With his bare hands.

He has gone out into the open fields
Superb, in final camouflage.

Michael Hinton

The Traveller

'Dust rose up then from the bandaged feet, shuffling,
Loaded the verminous clothes. Silent, an upward river,
Their haste was the less because they were going to death.

For them the clean brick building was arranged
Among the pine-trees, the toneless promise
Of shower-baths, the quiet closing
Of air-tight doors. That was no pleasant place.

And when, pierced from within, their worlds darkened,
The fake window, painted, was a new pain.
The others had painted it, the neat black-coated wardens,
Hoping, and so it was, that the people would be found
Gathered around it when the doors opened,
Unhindered by their bodies.

We, dear friends, as has often been said, were at the
    window,
And at the throwing of the switch, and at the burning,
And we have memories perhaps more clear than pleasant,
Unless our brains are now stones, which may be believed.

All this was both of two things, unsweet and unreasoned.
The cattle-trucks carried, singing, at the-turn of war-tide,
Jews and Gypsies, from the battle-fronts, hated people
Back to unspoken places; while, in sidings,
Held up, soldiers grumbled, rolled cigarettes,
Shells lay useless.
Reason might not urge this, stern word-rule,
So long as it spoke of things we knew. Understanding
Would show it as unwise, make it beyond the might
Of him who understood; he gains more worlds.
That this might be, there must be one of two things;
Either the casting aside of thought, heed to the blood's
    voice,

The shade-suggester, or the Reason they use
Who live in foreign places, darkening counsel
By words without knowledge, wandering in airy notions;
They use speech as it is not right to do.'

So spoke the traveller, and fell silent; a simple man.
His mind was troubled; he had sought peace with words.

Maurice Lindsay

London, September 1940

Helplessly the wavering searchlights probe
  where stuttering bombers fly:
each thud and flash their faceless pilots lob,
  anonymous numbers die,
shaking a length of protest from the ground:
  ack-ack guns chatter,
more distant heavies boom, and make resound
  the emptiness they batter.

Watching these beams meet in the cloudy blue
  of this unsummered night's
bewildered terror, foolishly, it's you
  who lingers in my sights,
eyes wide upon *Les Sylphides*. I remember
  you sitting at my side
through the uneasiness of that September
  when thought of peace died,
the sway of whiteness as the music dreamed
  what only music knows;
joy, more intense since it already seemed
  lost in our long-agos:
applause; the broken spell; cheer upon cheer
  for delicate civilisation,
as if the audience sensed that they'd been near
  some final consummation:
the heavy curtain tumbling from the ceiling;
  the glow of the house lights;
lifting a fur around your shoulders, feeling
  love must set all to rights:

helping you rise; the popping-back of your seat;
  a statue's marble stare;
your clinging little shudder as we met
  a coldly threatening air;
the newsboy hoarsely calling—*Hitler speaks*;
  the separating fear

of distance, blanched like powder on your cheeks
  at the mere thought of war . . .

Now it has happened. Searchlights take the sky,
and naked in another's arms you lie.

The Trigger

Only the trigger keeps him apart from Death;
to join their hands, I simply move my finger
and a bullet will pierce a hole in my enemy's breath.

Perhaps his breath would leak from him slowly, linger
a little, like air from a limply deflating balloon,
or the silence trailing the voice of a passionate singer,

and he would be still half-man, like the white morning
    moon
fading fainter under a blue cloth sky,
the end of living a longed-for, cursed-at boon;

till on a cushion of memories he would lie—
the shape of his young wife's mouth, his child's thin hair
how living emptied when one came to die!

Or it might all be over quickly, an affair
of absolute destruction; the heart ripped
or the brain scattered, quietly unaware.

And yet, if only my curling finger slipped
another would shake Death's casual welcoming hand
and follow on into his useless land;

a man who somehow is my enemy
would laugh and load again, and still be free.

Hugh MacDiarmid

from 'The Kind of Poetry I Want'

Yea, and with, and because of all this, the poetry
For which the poet at any moment may be smashed to pulp
By a gang of educated chimpanzees
Beating out the scansion with a rubber truncheon
For metronome on the small of his back
Till his kidneys burst—the poetry,
Not in Germany and certain other countries only,
But everywhere, England, Scotland, America,
The poetry of War and Civil War everywhere,
The poetry of the world-wide Night of the Long Knives
In which 99 men in every 100 are Gestapo Guards,
The poetry that entails the Family Trial
Of the poet's wife and children too,
And makes hulking Black Guards seize the Muses,
Tie their clothing tightly above their heads,
Truss, blind, shamefully humiliate them.
The Black Guards are among the helpless Muses now,
Beating them with clubs, kicking them in the guts,
The Black Guards carry on their dastardly work
While splitting their sides with laughter,
The Black Guards—Finance, Religion, Law, Capitalist
    Culture.
Himmler never moves a muscle—shows no pity
When, on his departure, frightful screams from the
    parade-ground
Tell of the most shameful deeds of all. . . . Next day
Ladies he meets at State functions
Are charmed by his quiet courtesy.
The poetry that is scheduled as a Dangerous Occupation,
The most dangerous occupation in the world to-day.
. . . Locked in a cell with a Luger pistol
I make my poetry of World Consciousness.
But will any of it ever be smuggled out
From the Sondergericht to which all Consciousness is
    subject
All over the world to-day?

Sondergericht: *the 'Special Court' (with no appeal) used by the Nazis to
control the population.*

Somhairle MacGill-Eain (Sorley MacLean)

Dol an Iar

Tha mi dol an iar san Fhàsaich
is mo thàmailt air mo ghuaillean,
gun d' rinneadh a' chùis-bhùrta dhìom
on a bha mi mar bu dual dhomh.

An gaol 's an t-iomrall bu mhotha,
an onair mheallta, mo mhilleadh,
le sgleò na laige air mo lèirsinn,
claonadh an èiginn a' chinne.

'S fhada bhuamsa an t-Eilean
is gealach ag èirigh air Catàra,
's fhada bhuam an Àird Ghiuthais
is rudhadh maidne air an Fhàsaich.

Tha Camas Alba fada bhuam
agus daorsa na Roinn-Eòrpa,
fada bhuam san Àird an Iar-thuath
na sùilean glas-ghorma 's bòidhche.

'S fhada bhuamsa an t-Eilean
agus gach ìomhaigh ghaoil an Alba,
tha gainmheach choigreach anns an Eachdraidh
a' milleadh innealan na h-eanchainn.

'S fhada bhuam Belsen 's Dachau,
Rotterdam is Cluaidh is Pràga,
is Dimitrov air beulaibh cùirte
a' bualadh eagail le ghlag gàire.

Tha Guernica fhèin glè fhada
bho chuirp neoichiontach nan Nàsach
a tha 'nan laighe ann an greibheal
's an gainmhich lachdainn na Fàsaich.

Chan eil gamhlas 'na mo chridhe
ri saighdearan calma 'n Nàmhaid
ach an càirdeas a tha eadar
fir am prìosan air sgeir-thràghad,

a' fuireach ris a' mhuir a' lìonadh
's a' fuarachadh na creige blàithe,
agus fuaralachd na beatha
ann an grèin theth na Fàsaich.

Ach 's e seo an spàirn nach seachnar,
èiginn ghoirt a' chinne-daonna,
's ged nach fuath leam armailt Roimeil,
tha sùil na h-eanchainn gun chlaonadh.

Agus biodh na bha mar bha e,
tha mi de dh'fhir mhòr' a' Bhràighe,
de Chloinn Mhic Ghille Chaluim threubhaich,
de Mhathanaich Loch Aills nan geurlann,
agus fir m' ainme—cò bu trèine
nuair dh'fhadadh uabhar an lèirchreach?

Going Westwards
translated by Sorley MacLean

I go westwards in the Desert
with my shame on my shoulders,
that I was made a laughing-stock
since I was as my people were.

Love and the greater error,
deceiving honour, spoiled me,
with a film of weakness on my vision,
squinting at mankind's extremity.

Far from me the Island
when the moon rises on Quattara,
far from me the Pine Headland
when the morning ruddiness is on the Desert.

Camas Alba is far from me
and so is the bondage of Europe,
far from me in the North-West
the most beautiful grey-blue eyes.

Far from me the Island
and every loved image in Scotland,
there is a foreign sand in History
spoiling the machines of the mind.

Far from me Belsen and Dachau,
Rotterdam, the Clyde and Prague,
and Dimitrov before a court
hitting fear with the thump of his laugh.

Guernica itself is very far
from the innocent corpses of the Nazis
who are lying in the gravel
and in the khaki sand of the Desert.

There is no rancour in my heart
against the hardy soldiers of the Enemy,
but the kinship that there is among
men in prison on a tidal rock

waiting for the sea flowing
and making cold the warm stone;
and the coldness of life is
in the hot sun of the Desert.

But this is the struggle not to be avoided,
the sore extreme of humankind,
and though I do not hate Rommel's army,
the brain's eye is not squinting.

And be what was as it was,
I am of the big men of Braes,
of the heroic Raasay MacLeods,
of the sharp-sword Mathesons of Lochalsh;
and the men of my name—who were braver
when their ruinous pride was kindled?

Curaidhean

Chan fhaca mi Lannes aig Ratasbon
no MacGillFhinnein aig Allt Èire
no Gill-Ìosa aig Cùil Lodair,
ach chunnaic mi Sasannach san Èipheit.

Fear beag truagh le gruaidhean pluiceach
is glùinean a' bleith a chèile,
aodann guireanach gun tlachd ann—
còmhdach an spioraid bu trèine.

Cha robh buaidh air 'san taigh-òsta
'n àm nan dòrn a bhith gan dùnadh',
ach leòmhann e ri uchd a' chatha,
anns na frasan guineach mùgach.

Thàinig uair-san leis na sligean,
leis na spealgan-iarainn beàrnach,
anns an toit is anns an lasair,
ann an crith is maoim na h-àraich.

Thàinig fios dha san fhrois pheilear
e bhith gu spreigearra 'na dhiùlnach:
is b' e sin e fhad 's a mhair e,
ach cha b' fhada fhuair e dh'ùine.

Chùm e ghunnachan ris na tancan,
a' bocail le sgreuch shracaidh stàirnich
gus an d' fhuair e fhèin mun stamaig
an deannal ud a chuir ri làr e,
beul sìos an gainmhich 's an greabhal,
gun diog o ghuth caol grànda.

Cha do chuireadh crois no meadal
ri uchd no ainm no g' a chàirdean:
cha robh a bheag dhe fhòirne maireann,
's nan robh cha bhiodh am facal làidir;
's co-dhiù, ma sheasas ursann-chatha
leagar mòran air a shàillibh
gun dùil ri cliù, nach iarr am meadal
no cop sam bith à beul na h-àraich.

Chunnaic mi gaisgeach mòr à Sasainn,
fearachan bochd nach laigheadh sùil air;
cha b' Alasdair à Gleanna Garadh—
is thug e gal beag air mo shùilean.

Heroes
translated by Sorley MacLean

I did not see Lannes at Ratisbon
nor MacLennan at Auldearn
nor Gillies MacBain at Culloden,
but I saw an Englishman in Egypt.

A poor little chap with chubby cheeks
and knees grinding each other,
pimply unattractive face—
garment of the bravest spirit.

He was not a hit 'in the pub
in the time of the fists being closed',
but a lion against the breast of battle,
in the morose wounding showers.

His hour came with the shells,
with the notched iron splinters,
in the smoke and flame,
in the shaking and terror of the battlefield.

Word came to him in the bullet shower
that he should be a hero briskly,
and he was that while he lasted
but it wasn't much time he got.

He kept his guns to the tanks,
bucking with tearing crashing screech,
until he himself got, about the stomach,
that biff that put him to the ground,
mouth down in sand and gravel,
without a chirp from his ugly high-pitched voice.

No cross or medal was put to his
chest or to his name or to his family;
there were not many of his troop alive,
and if there were their word would not be strong.
And at any rate, if a battle post stands,
many are knocked down because of him,
not expecting fame, not wanting a medal
or any froth from the mouth of the field of slaughter.

I saw a great warrior of England,
a poor manikin on whom no eye would rest;
no Alasdair of Glen Garry;
and he took a little weeping to my eyes.

Glac a' Bhàis

*Thuirt Nàsach air choreigin gun tug am Furair air ais do fhir
na Gearmailte 'a' chòir agus an sonas bàs fhaotainn anns an
àraich'.*

'Na shuidhe marbh an 'Glaic a' Bhais'
fo Dhruim Ruidhìseit,
gill' òg 's a logan sìos ma ghruaidh
's a thuar grìseann.

Smaoinich mi air a' chòir 's an àgh
a fhuair e bho Fhurair,
bhith tuiteam ann an raon an àir
gun èirigh tuilleadh;

air a' ghreadhnachas 's air a' chliù
nach d' fhuair e 'na aonar,
ged b' esan bu bhrònaiche snuadh
ann an glaic air laomadh

le cuileagan mu chuirp ghlas'
air gainmhich lachdainn
's i salach-bhuidhe 's làn de raip
's de sprùillich catha.

An robh an gille air an dream
a mhàb na h-Iùdhaich
's na Comannaich, no air an dream
bu mhotha, dhiùbhsan

a threòraicheadh bho thoiseach àl
gun deòin gu buaireadh
agus bruaillean cuthaich gach blàir
air sgàth uachdaran?

Ge b' e a dheòin-san no a chàs,
a neoichiontas no mhìorun,
cha do nochd e toileachadh 'na bhàs
fo Dhruim Ruidhìseit.

Death Valley
translated by Sorley MacLean

Some Nazi or other has said that the Führer had restored to German manhood the 'right and joy of dying in battle'.

Sitting dead in 'Death Valley'
below the Ruweisat Ridge,
a boy with his forelock down about his cheek
and his face slate-grey;

I thought of the right and the joy
that he got from his Führer,
of falling in the field of slaughter
to rise no more;

of the pomp and the fame
that he had, not alone,
though he was the most piteous to see
in a valley gone to seed

with flies about grey corpses
on a dun sand
dirty yellow and full of the rubbish
and fragments of battle.

Was the boy of the band
who abused the Jews
and Communists, or of the greater
band of those

led, from the beginning of generations,
unwillingly to the trial
and mad delirium of every war
for the sake of rulers?

Whatever his desire or mishap,
his innocence or malignity,
he showed no pleasure in his death
below the Ruweisat Ridge.

Latha Foghair

'S mi air an t-slios ud
latha foghair,
na sligean a' sianail mum chluasan
agus sianar marbh ri mo ghualainn,
rag-mharbh—is reòthta mur b' e 'n teas—
mar gum b' ann a' fuireach ri fios.

Nuair thàinig an sgriach
a-mach às a' ghrèin,
à buille 's bualadh do-fhaicsinn,
leum an lasair agus streap an ceathach
agus bhàrc e gacha rathad:
dalladh nan sùl, sgoltadh claistinn.

'S 'na dhèidh, an sianar marbh,
fad an latha;
am measg nan sligean san t-srannraich
anns a' mhadainn,
agus a-rithist aig meadhan-latha
agus san fheasgar.

Ris a' ghrèin 's i cho coma,
cho geal cràiteach;
air a' ghainmhich 's i cho tìorail
socair bàidheil;
agus fo reultan Afraga,
's iad leugach àlainn.

Ghabh aon Taghadh iadsan
's cha d' ghabh e mise,
gun fhaighneachd dhinn
cò b' fheàrr no bu mhiosa:
ar leam, cho diabhlaidh coma
ris na sligean.

Sianar marbh ri mo ghualainn
latha foghair.

An Autumn Day
translated by Sorley MacLean

On that slope
on an autumn day,
the shells soughing about my ears
and six dead men at my shoulder,
dead and stiff—and frozen were it not for the heat—
as if they were waiting for a message.

When the screech came
out of the sun,
out of an invisible throbbing,
the flame leaped and the smoke climbed
and surged every way:
blinding of eyes, splitting of hearing.

And after it, the six men dead
the whole day:
among the shells snoring
in the morning,
and again at midday
and in the evening.

In the sun, which was so indifferent,
so white and painful;
on the sand which was so comfortable,
easy and kindly;
and under the stars of Africa,
jewelled and beautiful.

One Election took them
and did not take me,
without asking us
which was better or worse:
it seemed, as devilishly indifferent
as the shells.

Six men dead at my shoulder
on an Autumn day.

Calum MacLeòid (Malcolm MacLeod)

El-Alamein

'S e nochd oidhch' a' bhatail mhóir,
'S tha gach aon againn air dòigh,
Le 'rifle' 's biodag thruist' nar dòrn
Air bruachan ciùin El-Alamein.

Tha 'n t-anmoch nis ri tarraing dlùth,
Tha ghealach togail ceann 's na niùil,
'S tha balaich chalma ri cur cùrs
Air tulaich àrd El-Alamein.

'S beag mo chàil bhith 'n seo an dràsd;
'S mór gum b' àill leam a bhith tàmh
An Eilean Leódhais le mo ghràdh
Fo sgàil Fir Bhréige Chalanais.

Ach siud am 'Fifty-first' an sàs,
Seòid na b' fheàrr cha deach gu blàr,
Na Siophorts, 's Camshronaich 's Earr-Ghàidheal
Cur smùid ast' le 'n cuid bhiodagan.

Tha nise seachdain agus còrr
Bho chuir mi na rainn-s' air dòigh,
'S tha Rommel le chuid Africa Corps
Air ruaig air falbh bho Alamein.

Cha robh bhuaidh bha siud gun phrìs,
Phàigh sinn oirr' le fuil ar crìdh';
Tha sinn fàgail mìltean sìnt'
San uaigh an ùir El-Alamein.

Chan eil an seo ach dùthaich thruagh,
Chan eil deoch innte na biadh;
'Bully beef' is brioscaid chruaidh,
'S e siud am biadh tha againne.

Bu shuarach leam bhith greis gun bhiadh,
Greis gun thàmh is greis gun dìon,
Ach tart ro mhór thug bhuam mo chiall
'S a dh'fhàg mi 'n-diugh ri fannachadh.

Is ged tha teas na fàsaich mhóir
Ga mo phianadh 's ga mo leòn,
Na faighinn-s' innte làn mo bheòil
De dh'uisge fuar cha ghearaininn.

Nan robh agam 'n seo an dràsd
Cothrom air an Tobair Bhàin,
Chan fhagainn i gu 'm biodh i tràight'
Ged bhiodh innt' na galanan.

El-Alamein
translated by John MacInnes

Tonight is the night of the battle
And each one of us is in good order,
With a rifle and bared bayonet in our hands
On the quiet braes of El Alamein.

It is now getting late;
The moon raises her head in the clouds,
And strong resolute men are setting a course
To the high mounds of Alamein.

Little my desire to be here just now;
I would much rather be resting
With my love in the Isle of Lewis
Underneath the shade of the Callanish Standing Stones.

But there's the 51st into action,
Better lads never went into battle:
The Seaforths, Camerons and Argylls
Wreaking havoc among them with their bayonets.

It is now a week and more
Since I put these verses together,
And Rommel with his Africa Corps
Is in flight from Alamein.

That victory was not without price—
We paid for it with our hearts' blood;
We are leaving thousands prostrate
In graves in the dust of Alamein.

This is but poor country
Without food or drink of its own;
'Bully beef' and hard biscuit,
That is the food we carry.

I am indifferent a while to being without food,
A while without rest or without shelter,
But the great thirst has taken my sense away,
Leaving me feebly fatigued.

And though the heat of the wide desert
Is paining and wounding me,
If I could only get a mouthful
Of cold water I would not complain.

But if I had here and now
One chance to get at the White Well,
I wouldn't leave her until she was dry
Though there are gallons upon gallons within her.

Colin McIntyre

Motor Transport Officer

Pyatt had something to do with horses.
No, that's not what I mean,
   wipe that smirk off your face.
I mean that in Civvy Street he had
   something to do with horses.
Not as a Trainer, you know, but in
   the buying and selling line.
A horse-chandler, or something.

We didn't have any horses in The Regiment,
   though we had some mules with us in Greece.
So we made him our Motor Transport Officer,
   as he was a Captain, and none of the other
   companies wanted him, not being a Gent.

He made a damn good transport officer, actually.
'Not afraid to get his head under the bonnet,'
   the Colonel always said.
And he could nurse a three-tonner back on the road,
   like a horse with an injured fetlock.

He didn't like the fighting much, and when shells
   fell, managed to be back with 'B' Echelon;
   and he drank too much.

But I wouldn't have wished his end, on man or beast.
Slewed a 15-hundredweight across the road, into a wall
   when he came upon a sudden roadblock.
Trapped in the cab, when the bastard truck caught fire.

Well, they shoot horses, don't they?

Infantryman

When you have walked through a town, as an infantryman
you'll never go through streets the same way again.

There is shoulder-ache from rifle-sling, and sore
butt-bruise, of bolt, on hip and thigh.

The walk comes somewhere between slope and slow hike,
a wary step, splay-footed, as drawers cellular,
catch in the crotch, twist centrifugally around.

Our lot moved at slow deliberate plod, eyes down, look out,
Ted walked on the left, looks right; I took the right,
looked left. Well spaced out, bloody tired all the time.

Ted and I had a reputation, in Four Section, for hitting
the deck, together, quick as a flash, at the first shell.
Ted had a nose for crossroads ranged by guns.

Infantrymen grow fat in later years, from never walking.
Ted would have become quite gross. But Ted's dead.
Stepped on an AP mine in champagne country.
Cheers, Ted, you old sod, you.

Naomi Mitchison

London Burning

London again, London burning again,
Again death and civilian pain.
Blitz talk on the side walk,
Foot steps on glass crunch,
Again phone calls in the morning:
Are you all right darling?
Again meeting at lunch
Roof spotters and rumour swappers.
Again importance of wardens
And again in train-jarred tunnels
The crammed pale shelterers
In from the snow's light flurry,
Warmer down below,
But the stuffed hours go slow
Living against the grain,
And we guess but cannot know
What breakfast time will show—
London again, was it London again?

Not like the old blitz, we say,
And up to noon, confident, almost gay,
Stick up our broken windows, plan, write, chatter,
Hope for news of friends, queue up for rations,
But by tea-time, even, night begins to matter.
Blankets in shelters, thermos filled, perhaps
Tonight might be quiet, perhaps only shrapnel,
Perhaps in a year's time it will be all a dream, perhaps.

Better get it over early. There it is. Those bloody sirens.
Get the babies out. Don't run, it'll be all right.
That's only barrage, only our own flares, go slowly.
Ruth, daughter-in-law, Ruth, where thou goest—
On the floor, in the small light of the torch, close over
    your baby:
If my body could shield you both from blast, take it,
Let the glass fangs bite me—But no, but no,
The thing I feel at my throat, that I will not show,

Is only my heart pattering, not London shaken
As the giants' hideous ball-game bangs overhead,
Banging no doubt over Berlin, does that comfort
Ourselves, or their bombs them, or is it something
From the implacable heavens, not to be avoided?—
If your number's there, it comes.
Shelterers of Europe, after the storm is over
We shall have this in common for our re-building,
Mortar of fear and endurance and a special laughter
And nightmare knowledge of the whistle that brings
    death.

Is it lightening? Yes, surely. Can we stand up?
Over for tonight. Pick up the babies. Did Anne get home?
Let's make tea. Gas pressure's low. And there's nothing
    like
A nice hot water bottle after a blitz.

London again, London burning again.
We were lucky that time the incendiaries dropped in the
    river;
But you can't expect such luck to last for ever.
London again.
Going to work tired, blitz talk in bus and office,
Re-filling buckets, blitz talk in shop and kitchen.
Going with a history book to a library,
Hoping to look up a reference,
Returning books to the library, there is no:
There is no library.

London again, London burning again,
Men and women, dog tired, asleep along the train,
Under familiar cosy slogans, Knightsbridge for Harrods,
    Green Park,
Piccadilly for Doughboys in the screamful dark:
Giggle and slap but half an eye on the time,
Get home, get in, get down, Big Ben's nine chime
And the news broken and the radio darting and stopping
And again the barrage and again the whistling dropping.
London again, London burning again.
Oh my city, my soul, city of the plain,
I, like Lot's wife, like Whittington, turn again.

Siren Night

Whoohoo go the goblins, coming back at nightfall,
Whoohoo go the witches, reaching out their hands for us,
Whoohoo goes the big bad wolf and bang go his teeth.
Are we sure we shall be the lucky ones, the princess, the
    youngest son,
The third pig evading the jaws? Can we afford to laugh?
They have come back, we always knew they would, after
    the story ended,
After the grown-ups shut the book and said goodnight.

When the windows went, Margaret was under the piano,
Bernice was behind the sofa. IT didn't see them.
At the third explosion Tony was under the bed clothes,
Hugging the hot water bottle. IT didn't see her either.
Next time IT might get any of us.
We had better be careful, better make the right gestures,
Better not laugh too much.

Whoohoo go the goblins, coming back to look for us.
The pale children are asleep in the Underground,
In the rabbit burrows, in the roots of goblin wood.
Whoohoo go the witches, stirring up the cauldron.
I can hear them now over our roof, can't you?
Wasp-wuzzing of the fly-king, the devil's own, high over
    London,
Round and round over the cauldron, sticks of noise
    stirring it.
Let us talk about something else. They may think we don't
    believe in them,
As the grown-ups didn't believe.

Let us shut the book on them. Let us switch on the
    gramophone.
Let us be rational, let us disbelieve in magic.
Countrymen of Handel and Haydn, countrymen of
    Beethoven,
You are not playing goblins, you are only wanting to kill
    us:
Wanting to frighten us. If you frighten us enough, you
    win.

We are a little frightened, we who have been happy,
We are not frightened enough to become what you want.
We set our will against yours, the will of London,
If you kill us, we only die.

Whoohoo go the goblins and cold, cold their fingers.
Some day the story will end, the book be shut for ever,
Sleep will be sweet again and sweet the waking,
There will be no more goblins.

We are only a little frightened.

The Farm Woman: 1942

Why the blue bruises high up on your thigh,
On your right breast and both knees?
Did you get them in the hay in a sweet smother of cries,
Did he tease you and at last please,
With all he had to show?
Oh no, oh no,
Said the farm woman:
But I bruise easy.

Why the scratched hand, was it too sharp a grip,
Buckle or badge or maybe nail,
From one coming quick from camp or ship,
Kissing as hard as hail
That pits deep the soft snow?
Oh no, oh no,
Said the farm woman:
But I bruise easy.

There was nothing, my sorrow, nothing that need be
    hidden,
But the heavy dung fork slipped in my hand,
I fell against the half-filled cart at the midden;
We were going out to the land.
Nobody had to know.
And so, and so,
Said the farm woman:
For I bruise easy.

The tractor is ill to start, a great heaving and jerking,
The gear lever jars through palm and bone,
But I saw in a film the Russian women working
On the land they had made their own,
And so, and so,
Said the farm woman:
And I bruise easy.

Never tell the men, they will only laugh and say
What use would a woman be!
But I read the war news through, every day;
It means my honour to me,
Making the crops to grow.
And so, and so,
Said the farm woman:
But I bruise easy.

William Montgomerie

The Edge Of The War (1939–)

On the esplanade
the deck-chair hirer
watches his summer
shovelled into sandbags
till at high tide
the beach is flooded to the Promenade

Our submarines like five alligators
pass
always at dusk
to the North Sea
where a German plane has sown surface mines

One mine circles the harbour slowly
missing the pier
again and again and again
until defused by a simple twist of the wrist

The whelk-seller leaves his bag and barrow
to pull a mine up the beach
and dies
'Stretchers! Stretchers here!'
they shout from the Castle

A policeman arrests one mine on the shore
and drags it halfway to the police-station
his tombstone a cottage gable-end
pocked with holes packed with red putty

Casks of brandy butter and ham
float on to the beach
from a mined ship

A grocer's van parks at dusk
by the Castle railings

Sergeant MacPherson pins on his notice-board
'Flotsam butter from the beach
must be left immediately
at the police-station'

For days the streets are sweet
with the smell of shortbread

Blue-mould butter
is dumped on the counter
or thrown at night
over the wall of the station
where greased door-handles will not turn

A German plane
following the wrong railway
dumps his bombs on an up-country farm

A plane from the North-Sea sunrise
machine-gunning our little fishing fleet
brushes a wing against a mast
and ditches

'Hilfe! Hilfe!'

'Take your time lads!'
shouts a skipper
to a drifter turning toward the sinking plane

'One of our planes
has sunk a German U-boat
off Montrose'

A war-rumour

The submarine
one of ours
dented
is in dry-dock
in Dundee

Bennet from Stratford-on-Avon
one of the crew
cycles to our house
with no lights
sings to us
of Boughton's Lordly Ones
from *The Immortal Hour*
talks of his wife in Stratford
and of the night they watched Birmingham burning

After late supper
he returns to the night
having left his ration of pipe-tobacco
on the piano

If his submarine sinks
he knows how to escape
and is found afloat
on the Pacific Ocean
drowned

On Tents Muir
across the Tay estuary
parachutes are falling
from war planes

We talk of the Second Front

One parachute does not open

Epitaph
For 2nd Officer James S. Montgomerie of the S.S. Carsbreck,
torpedoed off Gibraltar, 24th October 1941

My brother is skull and skeleton now
empty of mind behind the brow
in ribs and pelvis empty space
bone-naked without a face

On a draughty beach drifting sand
clawed by a dry skeleton hand
sifts in the hourglass of his head
time useless to bones of the dead

Thirty Years After

When you woke in the dark
listening from your bunk
to the ship's heartbeat
what fears came to you
from a boy's Glasgow
drowned deep in a man's memory
under curved dolphins
wide-winged gannets
floating isles of blae jellyfish
sea-fog
time-fused fears
deeper than nerve-ends of feeling
by day
beyond red and violet
by night
between dream and dream
between wave-bands of the ship's radio?

Still Hell under the keel
waked to terror
in a U-boat's crab eye
a torpedo between two waves
a bomb from a child's Heaven

Death with a razor
in this dark lane
ten-miles-of-rain wide
between our wiped windscreen
here in Spain
and brown beaches and Moroccan white houses in Africa
where nor'-west
Nelson waited for Villeneuve
where *Unterseebooten*
that night waited

                           *

Father looked up
that October night
from his black Bible
marked the place with conference notes
laid Book and pen
on the kitchen fender

You said
'I know this is my last voyage'

'Let's pray!' said father
kneeling
elbows on his armchair

In the morning
you caught the first tramcar to Glasgow Docks
with a suitcase of clean underwear
and father's Bible

By divine telepathy listening in
God removed Hell from under your keel
and in Heaven was joy
over one sinner repenting

In convoy by Land's End
by Finisterre
off duty you read your new Bible
between Cape St Vincent and Trafalgar
on the dark bridge hummed hymns
and timed the lighthouses

Here the nick-rhymed S.S. *Heartbreak*
broke
in a nightmare of decks tilting
alleyways at false angles
the rude sea entering all your exits

The dark night dipped you in baptism
in black water
with no blessing
in the name of Father Son Holy Ghost
no arm under your shoulder
in the Gospel Hall baptistry
no Brethren to sing resurrection

Only thanks from the Third Officer
for his life
and the crew rescued

Three bronze stars and silver medal
the bronze Atlantic Star
and Africa Star
the 1939–45 bronze star
the 1939–45 silver medal
with bright ribbons in a brown cardboard box

but nothing for the life you gave to save your crew

Edwin Morgan

from *The New Divan* (1977)

95

Slowly tawny, slowly ashy, the desert and the day
suddenly gulp the plum of darkness. Rays
of indigo spill down the wadis. Tents are cheerful
with lights-out laughter but the round of things is the
night. On guard, I climb the water-tower. Strengthening
stars are thick in absolute black. Who ever mourned
the sun? A universe unbroken
mends man and the dark. No northern mists envelop
me, there's nothing but the silent metal, the pack of stars
    from
zenith to horizon blazing down
on mile on mile of undulating sand. Swiftly
the thud of land-mines brings confusion
to the Canal. One star moves, drones. Position
on a map's the universe. The night is Rommel's tree:
searchlights cut it, history the secretion.

96

Paradise in prospect
after sand, after sand, after sand. Hungry
for vision yet thirsty for water, we're gleaming
sweaty ancient pilgrims that go softly
past mirages. With
thoughts withdrawn from emptiness
a while, we watch the flickering meadows.
Hedges of air that never flowered
flower, bands of dust that never moved
move now. Jinn's villages, different
from ours, the springs in their meadows
beckon dry as light. But we've come to
the casting-place, the arena we're in
shimmers with the real life still unseen.
A crone screws up her eyes. 'There,' she
points, 'in the east, the walls are white.'

97

Domes, shoeshines, jeeps, glaucomas, beads—
wartime Cairo gave the flesh a buzz,
pegged the young soul out full length,
made pharaohs in the quick electric
twilight, strutting brash as hawks. Underneath,
a million graves, a withered arm,
sarcophaguses red
with blood and ochre, smooth
boats on a dark sub-Nile
of slaves and captives, the
oldest way of gold,
over the dead with gold
and no haul of good.

98

You came under my mosquito-net
many times, till you were posted far off.
I was innocent enough
to think the posting was accidental.
When you left, it was my studious
avoidance of you that said goodbye.
It was enough; the body, not the heart.
We'd our black comedy too—
the night you got up, on Mount Carmel,
with a dog's turd flattened on your shirt-front:
not funny, you said.
Well, it was all a really unwashable laundry
that finally had to be thrown away.

99

I dreaded stretcher-bearing,
my fingers would slip on the two sweat-soaked handles,
my muscles not used to the strain.
The easiest trip of all I don't forget,
in the desert, that dead officer
drained of blood, wasted away,
leg amputated at the thigh,
wrapped in a rough sheet, light as a child,
rolling from side to side of the canvas
with a faint terrible sound
as our feet stumbled through the sand.

100

The dead climb with us like the living to the edge.
The clouds sail and the air's washed blue. For you
and me, the life beyond that sages mention
is this life on a crag above
a line of breakers. Oh I can't speak
of that eternal break of white, only of
memories crowding in from human kind,
stealthily, brazenly, thankfully, stonily
into that other sea-cave
of my head. Down where the breaker was
closes, darkens, rises, foams, closes; crates
drift across, whirl round
in the ghost of a gale;
a shred of sailcloth
relic of a gale
that really blew slews to the resting-place
the long tide goes out
to leave it, bleaching on its bony rock.
I pick it from the stone,
Hafiz, to bind the leaves of my divan.

Hafiz: *Morgan is addressing Hafiz, a fourteenth century Persian poet whose collected works—the* Divan—*reflect on love, beauty, sensuality and spirituality. These stanzas, with memories of Morgan's war-time desert service in the RAMC, conclude the long poem sequence.*

Edwin Muir

The River

The silent stream flows on and in its glass
Shows the trained terrors, the well-practised partings,
The old woman standing at the cottage gate,
Her hand upon her grandson's shoulder. He,
A bundle of clouts creased as with tribulations,
Bristling with spikes and spits and bolts of steel,
Bound in with belts, the rifle's snub-nosed horn
Peering above his shoulder, looks across
From this new world to hers and tries to find
Some ordinary words that share her sorrow.
The stream flows on
And shows a blackened field, a burning wood,
A bridge that stops half-way, a hill split open
With scraps of houses clinging to its sides,
Stones, planks and tiles and chips of glass and china
Strewn on the slope as by a wrecking wave
Among the grass and wild-flowers. Darkness falls,
The stream flows through the city. In its mirror
Great oes and capitals and flourishes,
Pillars and towers and fans and gathered sheaves
Hold harvest-home and Judgment Day of fire.
The houses stir and pluck their roofs and walls
Apart as if in play and fling their stones
Against the sky to make a common arc
And fall again. The conflagrations raise
Their mountainous precipices. Living eyes
Glaze instantly in crystal change. The stream
Runs on into the day of time and Europe,
Past the familiar walls and friendly roads,
Now thronged with dumb migrations, gods and altars
That travel towards no destination. Then
The disciplined soldiers come to conquer nothing,
March upon emptiness and do not know
Why all is dead and life has hidden itself.
The enormous winding frontier walls fall down,
Leaving anonymous stone and vacant grass.
The stream flows on into what land, what peace,
Far past the other side of the burning world?

Myra Schneider

Drawing a Banana
(A Memory of Childhood during the War)

Forty of us looked longingly at the yellow finger
Plumped, curved, bearing strange black marks.
The word 'banana' purred insistently round the classroom.
Our teacher, furrowed by severity as much as age,
Smiled slightly, then mounted her trophy on a box for us
To draw with thick pencil on thin, grey page.

We licked our lips in hope. Dimly we thought
The banana would be shared, perhaps that it would stretch
Like the bread and fish once did among the multitude.
A clearer idea flowered: it was for one child to win.
The bloom was nipped as it emerged our teacher meant to
    keep
The prize herself, and all alone to strip its golden skin.

It was boring drawing that banana. My leaden lines
Smudged with rubbings out didn't resemble the fruit
    taunting
My hungry eyes. I couldn't quite remember seeing
A 'live' banana before—there was a war to fight
And grown-ups said we had to go without and make do.
Yet if I closed my eyes I could conjure up a feast of a sight:

A window of violet-iced cakes and chocolates heaped
On silver trays belonging to a piece of magic time.
As far as my certainty stretched back war enveloped all.
War meant sombre ships sliding slowly down the Clyde,
Sirens, snuggling with cocoa in the cupboard beneath the
    stairs
Though the only bomb that fell was on the moors and no
    one died.

Fear couldn't touch me for I knew with crystal-cut clarity
Our side was in the right and therefore bound to win.
Yet my parents frowned and talked in hushed gloom
By the crackling wireless. If the Germans march through
    France
Never mind, I urged. With God fighting for England
It was in the fields of Hell that the fiend Hitler would
    dance.

I was proved right in the end, but long before then
My belief was crumbling in that lost paradise, peace.
I dreamed, daydreamed the war had ended. Warships
Decked out in scarlet streamers docked at our little pier,
Soldiers surged down the gangways to crowds in gaudy
    clothes,
Music reeled from radios—there'd be no more news to
    hear.

Ice-cream parlours would grow pink and come alive
To sell real ices not those fadings on the walls.
Rationing would end—I'd buy chocolate drops in mounds.
Bulging hands of bananas would hang in the greengrocer's
    shop
But instead of drawing stupidly I'd bite into a bunch
And no grim-faced grown-up would shout at me to stop.

Alexander Scott

Coronach
For the dead of the 5/7th Battalion, The Gordon Highlanders

Waement the deid
I never did,
Owre gled I was ane o the lave
That somewey baid alive
To trauchle my thowless hert
Wi ithers' hurt.

But nou that I'm far
Frae the fechtin's fear,
Nou I hae won awa frae aa thon pain
Back to my beuks and my pen,
They croud aroun me out o the grave
Whaur love and langourie and blyeness grieve.

Cryan the cauld words:
'We hae dree'd our wierds,
But you that bide ahin,
Ayont our awesome hyne,
You are the flesh we aince had been,
We that are bruckle brokken bane.'

Cryan a drumlie speak:
'You hae the words we spak,
You hae the sang
We canna sing,
Sen death maun skail
The makar's skill.

'Makar, frae nou ye maun
Be singan for us deid men,
Sing to the warld we loo'd
(For aa that its brichtness lee'd)
And tell hou the sudden nicht
Cam doun and made us nocht.'

Waement the deid I never did,
But nou I am safe awa
I hear their wae
Greetan greetan dark and daw—
Their wierd to sing, my wierd to dae.

The Sodgers

Nae wi the gallus captains
That niver jinkit war
But socht for glory's wildfire lowe
As wise men aince for anither star—

And nae wi the ramstam colonels
That leuch at the din o the drum
And skirled for the bleeze o battle's Inferno
As saunts micht skirl for Kingdom Come—

But aye wi the sweirt sodgers
That niver wished tae dee
And anelie marched the forrart road
Sen onie back they cudna see—

Near blind wi the reek o wappins
And the reek o leean words,
But niver near sae blind wi bluid
As faa in luve wi guns and swords.

Twa Images

I
The Twa Images

Twa images o doom
My terrors lour afore my een—
The t'ane I mind, and mindan cry *Forget!*,
The t'ither courie back frae in a dwaum,
But canna free mysel o either stoun.

II
The Image Minded

The keek-o-day a ruin's darklin corner
Wabbit in reek and haar,
The wabsters field-grey men,
Sae belted, banded, hung wi spikes o steel
(Gun-barrels, tripods, tools to howk the grund)
That nou, whan bullets dunt them doun
To hump and sprawl amang the aipple trees,
They're attercaps for aa that, iron airms upflung
For aa that their ain are faan and flat wi the mools.

Wabster mysel,
Sae belted, banded, hung wi spikes o steel,
I gaird a connached wab
The knotted neives o mortars blatter doun—
The raivelled wire,
The yirth aroun the grippit lips o the trenches
Gane splatteran starred like dubs ablow a stane,
The broken-backit snakes o smuke
Warsslan amang the aipple-trees
Whaur field-grey wabsters jink and rin and faa
In time til the bren-gun's habberan-hubberan tongue.

A spandau corncrakes frae its nest o haar
As a shouther jogs my ain,
I jerk my heid to see wha stands sae near me
And see him faa sae near me,
Backwart,

Thon shouther close to mine a hert-beat by
Gane closer yet to the grund,
And see, as he faas,
The burn o bluid that held him aince frae faain
Comes fountain-lowp
Frae whaur the bullet punched in's paper cheek
Thon hole sae smaa a farden's roun wad hap it—
Comes spout-o-scarlet up to the mirken air.

III
The Image Dreamed

Embro, a simmer day, the wind blawan,
Shakkan the licht like watter shook in a gless,
The North Brig in a single lowp
Frae scaur o stane to scaur o stane
Abune a howe that fumes wi reek,
And thonder ane whas face I canna see
Faain forever, faain doun and doun
Atween the scaurs,
Atween the windy lift and the reekan yirth,
Doun
And forever doun.

IV
The Images

Twa images o doom—
The lilt o my hert gaes hirplan lammiter slaw
At sicht o either,
But yet, though baith can teir my flesh
Wi the teeth o the same terror,
Their faces thraw in different frouns.

Mindan, I see the first ane mirrored,
Ilka detail Breughel'd back til the ee
Perjink and plain,
Frae runkles rived i the bark o the aipple-trees
To stour on a sodger's knuckles scrabblan the grund,
The haill reflection fact,
And terror thonder fact like aa the lave

As ane sae close—yet nae mysel—
Gaes backwart ower and doun
And out o the mirror.

Nae mirror, this, my second fear,
But etched on the bare lift in lines as bare,
The brig, the scaurs o stane, the wind blawan,
The reek ablow,
And ane whas face I canna see
Faain atween,
Nae mirror this, but melled frae myth and ferlie—

The brig's the North in Embro toun
And yet thon 'broken brig'
Whaur 'Babylon blaws by in stour,'
And look, thae columns heich on the Calton Hill
(A scaur o stane)
Are temple ower Troy,
And him that's faain doun and doun and doun,
The face I canna see,
He micht be Icarus
Or I.

North Brig: *this road bridge soars over Waverley Station, linking the old High Street with Princes Street in Edinburgh.*

broken brig: *from 'Song' by William Soutar (1898–1943).* 'Whaur yon broken brig hings owre; / Whaur yon water makes nae soun'; / Babylon blaws by in stour: / Gang down wi' a sang, gang doun.'

Calton Hill: *the National Monument, commemorating the Scottish dead of the Napoleonic Wars, was modelled on the Parthenon. Never completed ('Scotland's disgrace'), it stands on the Calton Hill overlooking Edinburgh, 'the Athens of the North'.*

Duncan Shaw

Pictures

These pictures I shall not forget:
A huddled group of weary refugees;
The high-piled trash upon the peasants' carts
An infant dead upon a harlot's knees;
The red dust on the roses, where a ruined house
Still, in grim mockery, bore a sign 'To Let';
The abandoned gardens; the deserted streets;
These I remember. Nor shall I forget
The painted pilot boat, twisted aslant
The severed hand that clutches the quayside dust;
The tears of an old French Commandant.
Nor shall the years so readily dispel
The remembered mockery of professed regret;
The blessing of the nun who smiled farewell;
Living, these pictures I shall not forget.

Sydney Goodsir Smith

from 'Armageddon in Albyn'

I. El Alamein

O, dearlie they deed
St. Valery's vengers
—The gleds dine weel
In the Libyan desert—
Dearlie they deed,
Aa the winds furthtell it.

Around El Alamein
Ranks o carrion
Faur frae their hame
Ligg sterk in the sun,
In the rutted sand
Whaur the tanks has run.

Yon burnan daw
Than dumb-deid blacker,
Whiter than snaw
Will the bricht banes glitter;
That this was for Alba
Maun we mak siccar!

It wasna for thraldom
Ye ligg there deid,
Gin we should fail ye
The rocks wad bleed!
—O, the gleds foregaither
Roun Alba's deid.

II. The Mither's Lament

Whit care I for the leagues o sand,
The prisoners an the gear they've won ?
Ma darlin liggs amang the dunes
Wi mony a mither's son.

Doutless he deed for Scotland's life;
Doutless the statesmen dinna lee;
But och tis sair begrutten pride
An wersh the wine o victorie!

III. The Convoy

The wind's on the Forth,
Icy the faem
Flicks at yir cheek—
A mirk thrang o ships
Is drawan hame.

Inby the room
Ma bairn hauds
Her breist lik a warld
In the lowe-licht; I staun
Neth the mune

An see the glib swaw
Til its aim heive an sweel
Ower aa the fields bleak
In sleep of our land,
Lik a gormaw.

Blawn clouds o reik
Fleer in the munelicht,
The lums hudder steep
Roun the shoreheid
And gaither like warlocks.

Heich i the caller lyft
White frae the mune-leam
The gulls mae lik weans
Then streek owre yir heid
Wi a deil's-screich.

Faur frae ma bairn
The maws' fey maen,
Nearer the fleet's hamein,
But aa connect, an
The plan agin's ain.

Mirk clouds frae the ships' stalks
Faur i the nicht-freith
Tell o harborie raucht—
Throu the cauld firth
The ships gang hamewith.

IV. The Sodjer's Sang

I deed in Greece
Whaur freedom liggs,
I deed in desert sand,
I deed maist aawhare
On the yerth
But in ma ain land.

They tell I deed
For libertie
But gin they speakna true
They'se pree the lees
O' a bitter bree
The sleepless deid shall brew.

V. Simmer Lanskip
A Sang for Bett

Aa simmer sings in the laden leaves
   Like molten pearls,
Mavis and laverock, lintie an merle
   Are carollan free,
   Are carollan free;
The fields whinner saft in a gowden swound,
   A peerie breeze
   In the sangrife tree
An roses' heavy scent around

   —But for the steel bird screams abune
   It micht be peace.

VI. Mars and Venus at Hogmanay

The nicht is deep,
The snaw liggs crisp wi rime,
Black an cauld the leafless trees;
Midnicht, but nae bells chime.

Throu the tuim white sleepan street
Mars an Venus shauchle past,
A drucken jock wi a drucken hure
Rairan 'The Ball o Kirriemuir'!

VII. *The War in Fife*

Gurlie an grey the snell Fife shore,
Frae the peat-green sea the cauld haar drives,
The weet wind sings on the wire, and war
Looks faur frae the land o Fife.

In ilka house tashed by the faem
Tuim beds tell o anither life,
The windae's blind wi the scuddan rain,
While war taks toll o the land o Fife.

By the 'Crusoe', backs tae the rain-straikit waa,
Auld jersied men staun hauf the day,
The fishing killt by trawlers, nou
They drink the rents the tourists pay.

But anither race has come, the pits
Breed a raucle fowk nae geck beguiles,
Deep in the yerth nae haar affects
The second war in the land o Fife.

Thae are the banded future; here
Dwine the auld defeated race;
Unseen throu the cauld an seepan haar
Destroyers slip at a snail's pace.

A foghorn booms athort the Forth,
Drumlie lament for a sundered life,
The root an flouer that aince were kith
Made strangers in the land o Fife.

The haar is chill, near in til the shore,
Nae maws screich owre the yalla freith,
The wireless frae a sweyan door
Ennobles horror, fire, an daith.

The foreign war tuims mony a bed
But yet seems faur awa—
Twa hunner years o Union's bled
The veins mair white nor ony war.

A third war cracks; lyart an loon
Thegither curse the lang stouthrife,
Mirk ower Scotland hings its rule
Like the snell haar hings ower Fife.

October 1941

Tchaikovski man, I'm hearan yir Waltz o Flouers,
A cry frae Russia fulls this autumn nicht;
Aa gousty fell October's sabban in ma room
As the frantic rammage Panzers brash on Moscow toun—
An the leaves o wud October, man, are sworlan owre the warld.

I' the gowden hairst o Forty-Ane the reid leaves drap, they
    whorl
Rain-dinged an spin frae the wund-thrawn creak o trees,
Lik tears o bluid they flee wi the airn tanks an drift athort,
Puir shauchlan shroud, the wae battallions o the deid—
O, the leaves o wud October, man, are sworlan owre the warld.

Outby ma winnock raggit branches drune
As roun the lums o Kiev, Warsaw, an the lave
O' sunken Europe; throu the wuids, by lochs, ablow the
    gastrous craigs
O' Caucasie, roads slip wi bluid mushed black wi leaves an
    rain—
O the tears o wud October, man, are sworlan owre the warld.

Trees greit their tears o bluid, they mell wi the bluid o
    men,
By a daft God's weirdless breith the fey leaves blawn aa
    widdershin
In the screich o whup or shell the grummlan wunds o
    daith,
This month bairned you an me, month o breme dualities,
    o birth an skaith—
O, the leaves o wud October, man, are sworlan owre the warld.

Sune rain wull freeze til snaw an the leaves be stilled
But yet thon oorie Deevil's Waltz'll straik the eastren
    fields,

Music o fa'an angels sab; maun aye the grey wunds blaw
An the drum o wounds aye dirl throu the smooran snaw?
*Aye, the leaves o wud October, man, are sworlan owre the
    warld.*

Whan Neva's black wi ice an glaizie in the mune-haar's
    lilly gleid
An trees drained black o tears, wull then the oorie sworl
Bide lown? Nae, chiel, tho dream ye maun o daw i the
    how-dumb-deid
The leaves o wud October, man, aye sworl across the warld.

Louise Findlay Stewart

The Sea-Wolf

The brown boats are sailing the wide seas tonight,
Looking doon is the moon wi' her deid face sae white.
The rim o' the sky is a' reddened wi' tears.
And the sea-mews are making a dirge o' their fears.

The wind's pipes are skirling 'Lochaber No More',
Oh! It's wae for the ones that are left on the shore;
Their hearts—like the sea's heart—are loupin' wi' fright
Looking doon is the moon wi' her deid face sae white.

Far, far are the bonnie brown boats frae the bay,
Cauld guests noo o' darkness and danger are they;
The Night Pack is hunting the lads' lives again—
Frae ruth o' the Sea-Wolf, Dear God, bield oor men.

William J. Tait

Tattoo (1938)

Through the dark thick air cleaves a cone of light
And, impinging on the screen, the news-reel comes to life:
The King at Lords, a train smash, the quarter-finals at
   Wimbledon,
And last, genteel emasculation, war in Spain.
Not the shambles at Badajoz, not the road
To Almeria, but the seige of San Sebastian
A century ago. Nor mud nor stench
Of putrefaction mars the glorious game.
The cannon vents its atrabilious spleen,
But spills no entrails on the well-kept lawn.
The musket's biting repartee evokes
No bouquets of blossoming bowels.
No fallen gladiator writhes,
Lips teeth-impaled and slobbering blood.
Each corpse drops wooden in the spot
Allotted it, the issue said
Ere one blank cartridge had been fired.
Behind, the cheering partisans, for once
All on the winner, proffer their applause.
On sweeps the fight and, closing hand to hand,
The gallant actors do and do not die.
The ramparts scaled, they bravely take the town,
'Encouraged,' says the commentator, 'by the cheers
Of thousands of blood-thirsty children.'

First Raid
(South Queensferry, 16th October, 1939)
A bus trip from Bo'ness to Edinburgh was interrupted to provide a grandstand view of the Forth Bridge air-raid.

The fall unseen, yet through the faces
The ripple washes and the question:
Doll necks jolt, a twist erases
The strident throbbing silence.

Answer, the blank air repossessed,
The still unpatterned blast and drone
Carried—dolls, jumble—to the crest
Of flux; the incredulous ebb.

Naked in the naked road,
'All in the blue unclouded weather'
Isolates herded by the goad,
Imminent, eye-defying.

Then tang and tingle change presage,
Immediate puppet to ultimate recorder;
Sun-gleam on streamlined fuselage,
Gay allotrope of fear.

Puffballs, squibs, toy ships and trains,
Juvenile but innocent;
The petulant flapping and steel rain
Mind-girders cannot bridge.

Yet blood peaks as the bomber stoops
Aslant the sky: exhaust crescendo,
Mad drum tattoo, the eyes still dupes
Of the aerial pageant.

The fall revealed, slow past belief,
The midget bomb incordinately fraught:
Gap-gasp in living, lung-relief
In the shattering saving roar of the explosion.

Ruthven Todd

The Drawings for Guernica

The woman weeps forever as if her tears
Would wash away the blood and broken limbs,
And the tortured horse whinnys and climbs
Iron hoof on broken beam towards electric stars.
Hands hold withered flowers, the broken sword
And the great arm reaches out with a lamp.
The frightened child in its mother's clasp is limp,
Too terrified to listen to the comfortable word.

Still the great bull stands inside the shattered room,
Inside the world, and still the crouching woman runs
Feeling the child moving in her tightened womb,
Thinking of the small features and the forming bones.
Shut in forever by the grey wall the woman weeps
While the mad horse plunges up the useless slopes.

It Was Easier

Now over the map that took ten million years
Of rain and sun to crust like boiler-slag,
The lines of fighting men progress like caterpillars,
Impersonally looping between the leaf and twig.

One half the map is shaded as if by night
Or an eclipse. It is difficult from far away
To understand that a man's booted feet
May grow blistered walking there, or a boy

Die from a bullet. It is difficult to plant
That map with olives, oranges or grapes,
Or to see men alive at any given point,
To see dust-powdered faces or cracked lips.

It is easier to avoid all thought of it
And shelter in the elegant bower of legend,
To dine in dreams with kings, to float
Down the imaginary river, crowds on each hand

Cheering each mention of my favoured name.
It is easier to collect anecdotes, the tall tales
That travellers, some centuries ago, brought home,
Or wisecracks and the drolleries of fools;

It is easier to sail paper-boats on lily-ponds,
To plunge like a gannet in the sheltered sea,
To go walking or to chatter with my friends
Or to discuss the rare edition over tea,

Than to travel in the mind to that place
Where the map becomes reality, where cracks
Are gullies, a bullet more than half-an-inch
Of small newsprint and the shaped grey rocks

Are no longer the property of wandering painters,
A pleasant watercolour for an academic wall,
But cover for the stoat-eyed snipers
Whose aim is fast and seldom known to fail.

It is easier . . . but no, the map has grown
And now blocks out the legends, the sweet dreams
And the chatter. The map has come alive. I hear the moan
Of the black planes and see their pendant bombs.

I can no longer hide in fancy: they'll hunt me out.
That map has mountains and these men have blood:
'Time has an answer!' cries my familiar ghost,
Stirred by explosives from his feather bed.

Time may have answers but the map is here.
Now is the future that I never wished to see.
I was quite happy dreaming and had no fear:
But now, from the map, a gun is aimed at me.

These Are Facts

These are facts, observe them how you will:
Forget for a moment the medals and the glory,
The clean shape of the bomb, designed to kill,
And the proud headlines of the paper's story.

Remember the walls of brick that forty years
Had nursed to make a neat though shabby home;
The impertinence of death, ignoring tears,
That smashed the house and left untouched the Dome.

Bodies in death are not magnificent or stately,
Bones are not elegant that blast has shattered;
This sorry, stained and crumpled rag was lately
A man whose life was made of little things that mattered.

Now he is just a nuisance, liable to stink,
A breeding-ground for flies, a test-tube for disease:
Bury him quickly and never pause to think
What is the future worth to men like these?

People are more than places, more than pride;
A million photographs record the works of Wren;
A city remains a city on credit from the tide
That flows among its rocks, a sea of men.

Sydney Tremayne

Elegy

Putting aside the drums, the plumes, the hymns,
all grief's dark luxury,
I make this unheroic elegy
for friends and foemen slain.

No organ chariot shall bear me from them.
I draw towards them softly
as the dusk. If in the dusk stars rise,
I seek one only. Now
humbly and like a lover who does not hope
I plead alone with the night
that truth may not pass by in a wind of words.

No love can reach them now.
Nothing can heal but time and our forgetting.
Time will forget, but now
they are newly gone. Our words call after them,
though we cannot made amends. We cannot mend
the love that suddenly stopped,
the private dream of freedom that bled away.

The girls are dressed in black,
the children cry, and play with the new toy,
the better job is filled,
the house is sold. The photo behind the clock
is yellow and out of date.
The heart of hate is cooled; the whispered tick
has drowned the battle's shout.
And what is freedom? Ask the circling hands;
they answer with a cipher:
minutes, hours, and years, the shape of worlds.

These men were frail deepest in their desiring.
They sought peace in certain people
and certain places. The ribs of longing cracked
at a chance word's weight.
Love was a cur slinking beside their feet
that had no heart for freedom.
Peace was their lifesought land, their pole and positive.

It was not peace they found
far from their homes, or under their ruined homes
when the sky fell and the ground
was gashed and gaped for steeples that told their time.
When the clocks fell down they died:
they were rid of rest, of right, of reason, of love
and above their heads no hope.
The living alone knew loss and the need to act,
the gruesome bin, the debris of bone and dream.

The living cleaned up the mess,
dirtied among debris, hating the fate of flesh,
sickened to hardness, broken
to burial's chores. But they could not bury their loss;
loss was alive in the belly,
aching its independence, assured of birth.

Looted of life, lost,
names drop like stones in pools of loneliness
and sorrow's circles widen.
Taking themselves away, what could they give?
O blind and bitter love,
we have your pledge: dead victories, living loss.

From this defeat what grows?
They care no more. Unless the living care
there is only the striding clock
to keep its recurrent rendezvous with fear,
we'll sing a hymn, erect a monument,
place contracts for barbed wire.

Douglas Young

Leaving Athens
2nd September, 1939

Parnes, Pentelikon, Hymettos, glowing
rose-red with sunset, violet waters flowing
    north from the stern, long furrows outward whitening—
this twilit coolness soothes our troubled going.
    Through the hot day new rumours vague and frightening
of ruinous war alarmed us, never knowing.

Now with light hearts our Odyssey is started
into a sea of dangers yet uncharted.
    There may be peace for all the war-storm's blackening.
Remember how Odysseus, lion-hearted,
    passed through a hundred perils without slackening,
and found his home as safe as when he parted.

More likely home to ruins. That old jurist
Servius Sulpicius Rufus, as a tourist
    among the wrecks of Greece serenely pondering,
wrote to his Cicero what seemed the surest
    anodyne for his grief. And in our wandering
we have a consolation, not the poorest.

Nos homunculi indignamur si quis nostrum interiit aut occisus est,
quorum vita brevior esse debet, cum uno loco tot oppidum cadavera
projecta jaceant?

The carcases of ancient cities lying
may teach a man the smallness of his dying.
    Berlin and Warsaw bombed, and men in chiliads
shattered and choking—legless children crying
    round headless mothers—themes for modern Iliads!
Some gas-blind Homer hymn the bombers' flying!

Horrors may turn to beauty. Not despairing
of human progress, nor too greatly caring
    how soon or how, we watch the myriad mystery.

Ruin of empires, cities skyward flaring,
    massacred millions, mark the march of History.
Success will crown at last Man's skill and daring.

Enough of Stoicism, enough of moping.
Enjoy the limestone ridges seaward sloping,
    the moonlit surges and the white gulls' hovering.
After long months' uncertainty and groping
    for peace and safety, now at last uncovering
the face of war we smile and go on hoping.

Nos homunculi . . . 'Shall we poor mortals be indignant if one of us dies
or is slain, when our lives ought rather to be shorter than they are, since
the skeletons of so many towns lie prostrate and neglected on one
spot?'—Servius Sulpicius in a letter of condolence to Cicero on the
occasion of his daughter's death.

For Alasdair

Standan here on a fogg-yirdit stane,
drappan the bricht flees on the broun spate,
I'm thinkan o ye, liggan thonder your lane,
i the het Libyan sand, cauld and quate.
    The spate rins drumlie and broun,
    whummlan aathing doun.

The fowk about Inverness and Auld Aberdeen
aye likeit ye weel, for a wyce and a bonny man.
Ye were gleg at the Greekan o't, and unco keen
at gowf and the lave. Nou deid i the Libyan sand.
    The spate rins drumlie and broun,
    whummlan aathing doun.

Haiddan the Germans awa frae the Suez Canal,
ye dee'd. Suld this be Scotland's pride, or shame?
Siccar it is, your gallant kindly saul
maun lea thon land and tak the laigh road hame.
    The spate rins drumlie and broun,
    whummlan aathing doun.

fogg-yirdit: *moss-covered.*
the laigh road: *by which the dead travel.*

Biographical Notes

Marion Angus (1865–1946)
Born in Sunderland of Scottish parents, Angus spent her formative years in Arbroath where her father was a minister in the Free Church. Before the First World War she ran a private school with her sister in Cults, and during the war she volunteered for work in the canteen of Stobbs camp. Angus exerted a strong influence on the Scottish literary renaissance, publishing six volumes of poetry in Scots between 1922 and 1937 and featuring in Hugh MacDiarmid's *Scottish Chapbook* and *Northern Numbers*.

J. K. Annand (1908–1993)
Born and educated in Edinburgh, Annand trained as a teacher and, inspired by MacDiarmid's example—a former pupil of Broughton School, like himself—he took up the cause of poetry in Scots. As well as founding *Lallans* the Scots language journal in 1973, he published Scots rhymes for children and translations from German and medieval Latin. He served in the Royal Navy during the war.

Archibald Allan Bowman (1883–1936)
Educated at Beith Academy and Glasgow University, Bowman was the holder of the Stuart Chair in Logic at Princeton University at the outbreak of the First World War. He enlisted in 1915, receiving a commission in the 13th Highland Light Infantry. Bowman was taken prisoner during the Battle of Lys in April 1918, and was imprisoned at Rastatt and Hesepe prison camps. He returned to Glasgow University in 1925 taking up the Chair in Logic and Rhetoric, and in 1926 the Chair in Moral Philosophy.

Edward Boyd (1916–1989)
Born in Ayrshire, Boyd worked as stage manager, actor and director for Glasgow Unity Theatre in the 1940s. He served in the RAF during the war and returned to civilian life as the author of children's books, and then as a radio and TV script writer, best known for his contributions to *Z Cars* and the creation of *The View From Daniel Pike*, starring Roddy MacMillan.

John Buchan (1875–1940)

Writer, publisher, lawyer, administrator, and politician, Buchan was born in Perth, educated in Fife and Glasgow, and spent many formative summers in Broughton in the Borders. He attended Glasgow and Oxford Universities and worked as a colonial administrator in South Africa in the aftermath of the Boer War. In the First World War, Buchan was a director of the Edinburgh publisher Nelsons, for whom he wrote the twenty-four-volume *Nelson's History of the War*, and was an officer in the Intelligence Corps and Director of the Department of Information. He maintained a prolific output of fiction and non-fiction after the war, was Unionist MP for the Scottish Universities (1927–1935), and became, as Baron Tweedsmuir of Elsfield, governor-general of Canada (1935–1940).

Norman Cameron (1905–1953)

Born in Bombay, Cameron was educated at Edinburgh and Oxford. He worked in Intelligence, producing propaganda during the war, and served in Austria until 1947, before returning to civilian life to work in advertising. He contributed to Geoffrey Grigson's *New Verse* in the 1930s, and the Hogarth Press published his slim volume of *Collected Poems* in 1957.

William Cameron (dates unknown)

A contributor to the Glasgow Socialist newspaper, *Forward*, edited by Thomas Johnston. The paper took a strong anti-war stance before and during the First World War and was, for a time in 1916, suppressed for its dissidence.

R. W. Campbell (1876–?)

Robert Walter Campbell was a prolific and popular novelist, best known for his Spud Tamson series, *Private Spud Tamson* (1915), *Sergeant Spud Tamson, VC* (1918), *Spud Tamson out West* (1924), and *Spud Tamson's Pit* (1926) as well as a number of broadly propagandistic wartime novels and romances. He served in the Boer War with the Royal Scots Fusiliers, and returned from the Special Reserve to serve as a captain in the regiment in the First World War. He served at Gallipoli before returning to the reserve in 1916.

W. D. Cocker (1882–1970)

Cocker was born in Rutherglen. He left school at thirteen to work for the *Daily Record* before serving in the First World War with the 9th Highland Light Infantry and, from 1915, the Royals Scots. He was taken prisoner in 1917 and was held at Enger, near Minden. After the war he returned to the world of journalism, becoming a well-known figure on the *Daily Record* and its sister paper the *Evening Times*, accruing over fifty years of service with them. He became known between the wars for his poems in Scots, particularly those about the Strathkendrick area, and was president in the 1940s of the Glasgow Ballad Club.

George Sutherland Fraser (1915–1980)

Fraser was born in Glasgow and brought up in Aberdeen. He studied at St Andrews University and served with the army in Cairo where he was published as one of the *Salamander* poets. He supported the 'New Apocalypse' literary movement, although his own urbane and often epistolary poems were not in that vein. After the war he became a noted journalist and critic in London literary circles.

Olive Fraser (1909–1977)

Born in Aberdeen and brought up by a great-aunt, Fraser was educated at Aberdeen University and Girton College, Cambridge. She was troubled by frail mental and physical health all her life (much later found to be an undiagnosed hyperthyroid condition) and although she won the Chancellor's Medal for poetry in 1935 her creative career was not a happy one. When war broke out she was posted to watch duty in Liverpool during the heavy air raids of May 1941, an experience that led to her being released on compassionate grounds. After the war she lived in the South before returning to Aberdeen in the 1960s. Her collected poems were published posthumously in 1989.

Robert Garioch Sutherland (1909–1987)

Born and educated in Edinburgh, and trained as a schoolteacher, Garioch was conscripted into the Royal Signal Corps in 1941, only to be captured the following year by German troops during Operation Torch, the allied invasion of French North West Africa. He described his time as a

POW in *Two Men and a Blanket* (1975) although the experi-
ence also coloured the visionary horror of his long poem,
The Wire. After a few years in London he returned to Edin-
burgh, to work for the rest of his life as a teacher and a
poet.

Flora Garry (1900–2000)

Born in the Aberdeenshire countryside, Flora Campbell
graduated from Aberdeen University and worked as a
schoolteacher in the North East before marrying Robert
Garry who later became a professor of medicine in Glasgow.
Flora wrote stories and plays for the radio during the 1920s,
but did not begin to write poetry until the Second World
War broke out. Best known for poetry in her native
Buchan Doric, she also wrote in English although her work
was not published in book form until the appearance of
Bennygoak and Other Poems in 1975.

Jack Gillespie (1909–2012)

Born to Scottish parents in Liverpool, Gillespie was a peace-
time territorial soldier, joining the Queen's Own Cameron
Highlanders when war broke out. He served in North Africa,
Italy, Sicily, Bulgaria and Austria, writing poems to enter-
tain his fellow soldiers, collected in *The Poetic Journal of a
Cameron Highlander* to mark his one hundredth birthday in
2009.

Deorsa Mac Iain Deorsa, George Campbell Hay (1915–1984)

Born in Renfrewshire, the son of novelist John MacDougall
Hay, Hay was brought up in Tarbert, going to school in
Edinburgh and then to Oxford University. To evade con-
scription (he was a passionate Scottish nationalist) he fled
to Argyll before being caught, imprisoned and eventually
recruited to the Royal Army Ordinance Corps. A gifted lin-
guist and translator, he served in North Africa (where he
witnessed the bombing of the Tunisian town of Bizerta),
Italy and Macedonia. His wartime experiences, including a
beating he suffered in Macedonia for being too friendly
with the local people, marked him for life. His poetry, in
Gaelic, Scots and English, is equally marked by his compas-
sion for the suffering poor of the world.

John MacDougall Hay (1881–1919)

The author of the novel *Gillespie* (1914), MacDougall was a minister of the Church of Scotland and occasional freelance writer. He was born in Tarbet, Loch Fyne and educated at Glasgow University where he took a degree in arts in 1901. He worked as a teacher in Stornoway and Ullapool before returning to Glasgow in 1908 to train for the ministry. He was a minister in Govan before settling in a parish in Elderslie. He died of tuberculosis in 1919.

Hamish Henderson (1919–2002)

Born in Blairgowrie to a single mother, scholarships gave Henderson an education in London and Cambridge. Strongly left-wing in his views, when war broke out he joined the Pioneer Corps before taking a commission in Army Intelligence to serve in the North African desert war and the invasion of Italy. His experiences at El Alamein gave rise to the major poem sequence *Elegies for the Dead in Cyrenaica* (1947). He also wrote songs, ballads and satirical poems about army life and went on to become a leading scholar in the School of Scottish Studies and the folk revival in Scotland in the 1950s and 1960s.

James Findlay Hendry (1912–1986)

Born in Glasgow, Hendry studied at Glasgow University and—like G. S. Fraser, and Henry Treece—was a proponent of and contributor to the New Apocalypse poetic movement of the later 1930s. He served in the Royal Artillery and Army Intelligence during the war, publishing two collections in the early 1940s. After the war he travelled the world as a professional translator, and eventually moved to Canada. He produced the fine novel *Fernie Brae* (1947), a life of Rilke (1982) and two more collections of poetry in 1978 and 1980.

Michael Hinton (dates unknown)

We have not been able to trace Hinton, but his poem 'The Traveller' speaks for how the news about the German concentration camps impacted on this young student at St Andrews. His poem was published in *Scottish Student Verse 1937–1947*, introduced by Eric Linklater.

Violet Jacob (1863–1946)
A novelist and poet, and one of the leading lights of the Doric revival, Violet Jacob was a sister of the Laird of Dun. She married an army officer and spent much of her life in postings in India, Egypt, and England, writing all the time of the landscapes and people of Angus. Her only son, Harry, was killed, aged twenty-one, at the Battle of the Somme. She settled in Kirriemuir following the death of her husband in 1936.

Roderick Watson Kerr (1893–1960)
Edinburgh-born, Kerr served as a lieutenant in the First World War in the 2nd Royal Tank Corps. He was wounded and won the MC during the German Spring Offensive in March 1918. Following the war he worked as a journalist at the *Scotsman* and, from 1926, as a leader writer at the *Liverpool Daily Post*. He was co-founder, with George Malcolm Thomson, of the Porpoise Press in 1922.

Joseph Lee (1876–1949)
A poet, journalist, and illustrator, Lee was born and educated in Dundee. He left school aged fourteen, working as a solicitor's clerk and then travelling the world as stoker on steamships and working as a cowpuncher in Canada, before returning to a career as a journalist in Dundee. He enlisted as a private in the Black Watch in 1914, rising to the rank of sergeant, and in 1917 received a commission in the 10th King's Royal Rifle Corps. He was captured in 1917 and imprisoned at Carlsruhe. He returned to a career in journalism after the war.

Maurice Lindsay (1918–2009)
Born and educated in Glasgow, Lindsay joined up as a Captain with the Cameronians when war broke out and served as an advisor to the War Office in London. These years are remembered in the early chapters of his autobiography *Thank You for Having Me* (1983). He published several collections during the 1940s and continued to produce poetry for the rest of his life. After the war he returned to Scotland to work as an influential editor, critic and broadcaster speaking as a moderate voice in support of Scottish poetry and the Scottish literary revival.

W. S. S. Lyon (1887–1915)

Walter Scott Stuart Lyon was born in North Berwick and educated at Balliol College, Oxford. He was an Advocate at the Scottish Bar, before volunteering in 1914 and serving as a lieutenant in the 9th Battalion the Royal Scots. He was killed during the Second Battle of Ypres in 1915. The proceeds of his posthumously published *Easter at Ypres 1915, and other* poems went to the Edinburgh University Settlement, of which he had been Sub-Warden.

MacKenzie MacBride (dates unknown)

A popular author of, among others, *Wonderfu' Weans* 1903, *Arran of the Bens, the Glens and the Brave* 1910, and *With Napoleon at Waterloo* 1911. MacBride's collection of patriotic verses, *For Those we Love at Home! and Other War Songs and Ballads* was published in 1916.

Hugh MacDiarmid (1892–1978)

Born in Langholm, and imbued with what he took to be a Borderer's combativity, Christopher Murray Grieve served with the RAMC in Salonika during the First World War. By the 1920s he had set the Scottish literary renaissance in motion as a convinced nationalist, a life-long socialist, and a brilliant, controversial and prolific poet. He was conscripted for war work in 1942 and served as a munitions fitter and then aboard a supply boat in industrial Clydeside. Committed to international socialism and a new conception of depersonalised epic verse, his poetry says almost nothing about his own experience during these years.

Dòmhnall Ruadh Chorùna, Donald MacDonald (1887–1967)

North Uist-born, MacDonald served in the militia before enlisting in the Camerons at the outbreak of the First World War. He was seriously wounded in the Battle of the Somme in 1916 and subsequently served with the West Riding Field Regiment. He returned to Uist to become a stonemason. His poems and songs existed for a long time only in oral form until they were taken down from his dictation shortly before his death and subsequently published in two volumes, *Dòmhnall Ruadh Chorùna*, edited by John Alick Macpherson (1969) and Fred Macaulay (1995).

Patrick MacGill (1889–1963)

From Glenties in Donegal, MacGill emigrated to Scotland as a teenager, coming to literary notice through selling door-to-door in Greenock his self-published *Gleanings from a Navvy's Scrapbook* (1911). His reputation was made with the publication of the autobiographical *Children of the Dead End* (1914) and *The Rat-Pit* (1915), which detailed in lightly fictionalised form the experiences of Irish immigrants in Glasgow. He enlisted with the London Irish Rifles in 1914, serving as a stretcher-bearer. MacGill was wounded and gassed during the Battle of Loos in 1915, being invalided to the UK where he later worked in the Intelligence Department of the War Office. In addition to his *Soldier Songs* (1917) he produced three prose memoirs of the war, *The Amateur Army* (1915), *The Great Push* (1916) and *The Red Horizon* (1916).

Pittendrigh MacGillivray (1856–1938)

Known principally as a sculptor, James Pittendrigh MaGillivray's poetic experiments encompassed English, Doric and Lowland Scots. Born in Inverurie, Aberdeenshire, he trained with William Brodie in Edinburgh and with Glasgow sculptor John Mossman before settling in Edinburgh in 1894. His sculptures include the Burns statue in Irvine, the Gladstone monument in Edinburgh, and the statue of John Knox in St Giles Cathedral, Edinburgh. He was an associate of the Glasgow Boys and a co-founder of *The Scottish Arts Review*.

E. A. Mackintosh (1893–1917)

Born in Brighton to a Scottish father and English mother, Ewart Alan Mackintosh was educated at Brighton College, St Paul's School, and Christ Church Oxford. He left his studies in Greats at Oxford to volunteer at the outbreak of the First World War, gaining a commission in December 1914 in the Seaforth Highlanders. He served in France from July 1915, winning the Military Cross, before he was wounded and gassed at High Wood during the Battle of the Somme in 1916. He returned to France in September 1917 and was killed in November of that year at Cambrai.

Somhairle MacGill-Eain, Sorley MacLean (1911–1996)

Born on the island of Raasay, MacLean studied at Edinburgh University and trained as a teacher. It was during these years that he confirmed his strongly socialist beliefs and found an affinity with MacDiarmid's campaign for a Scottish cultural and linguistic revival—most especially, in his case, for a fully modern poetry in Gaelic. His concerns about the Spanish Civil War and an unhappy love life led to the major poems collected as *Dain do Eimhir* (1943). When war broke out MacLean served as a member of the Signals Corps in North Africa, where he was severely wounded at El Alamein.

Calum MacLeòid, Malcolm MacLeod (dates unknown)

From the Isle of Lewis, MacLeod (nickname Calum Cuddy) was brought up in a croft house near the standing stones of Callanish. He served in North Africa with the Seaforth Highlanders, 51st Highland Division.

Colin McIntyre (1927–2012)

Born in Argentina of Scottish parents, McIntyre returned to the UK at the age of seventeen to be commissioned in the Black Watch, his father's old regiment, at the very end of the war. He served with the Lovat Scouts in Greece and the 6th Airborne Division in Palestine.

Hamish Mann (1896–1917)

Educated at George Watson's College, Edinburgh, Mann was gazetted as a second lieutenant in the 8th Black Watch in July 1915. He fought in the Battle of the Somme and was killed leading his platoon in the Battle of Arras in April 1917.

Naomi Mitchison (1897–1999)

Born in Edinburgh to the distinguished Haldane family, Mitchison's student days at Oxford were interrupted by the First World War, during which she served as a voluntary nurse. She married the barrister Dick Mitchison in 1916 and went on to make a career for herself as a novelist, a journalist, and a socialist activist throughout the thirties, a campaigner for family planning and women's rights and a leading light in Bohemian London literary circles. She was living at her house in Carradale when war broke out in 1939. She worked hard to farm the land there, but kept her contacts with regular visits to London.

William Montgomerie (1904–1994)
Born and educated in Glasgow, Montgomerie did not follow in his father's footsteps as a member of the Plymouth Brethren. He worked as a schoolteacher in Dundee, and became, with his wife Norah, a keen collector of Scottish rhymes, ballads and folk poetry. He lost two brothers during the war.

Edwin Morgan (1920–2010)
Born in Glasgow, Morgan was a student at Glasgow University when he was called up. His beliefs as a conscientious objector allowed him to serve as a private from 1940 to 1946 in the Royal Army Medical Corps. As part of the North African campaign, he was stationed at military hospitals at El Ballah, the Lebanon and Haifa. After the war he graduated and went on to work as a lecturer and ultimately as a professor at the University of Glasgow. He became one of Scotland's best-known and best-loved poets. It was over twenty years before he began to reflect on his wartime years in his poetry.

Edwin Muir (1887–1959)
Born and brought up in Orkney, modern industrial city life came as a shock to the young Muir when his family moved to Glasgow in 1901. He lived and travelled in Europe during the twenties, and began his career as a poet, critic and novelist, and with his wife Willa, a translator of German literature. The family lived in St Andrews and Edinburgh during the war years, before Muir's contacts took him abroad again, as Director of the British Council in Prague and Rome, before becoming warden of Newbattle Abbey outside Edinburgh and latterly a professor at Harvard.

Iain Rothach, John Munro (1889–1918)
Born in Lewis and educated there and at Aberdeen University, Munro volunteered at the outbreak of the First World War. He served in the ranks in the 4th Seaforth Highlanders from 1914 before being commissioned as a Second

Lieutenant in June 1916. He won the Military Cross and was killed in action at Ploegsteert in Flanders on 16 April 1918 during the German Spring Offensive.

Neil Munro (1863–1930)
Best known for his humorous stories of Glasgow and the West Coast, featuring Erchie MacPherson, Jimmy Swan, and Para Handy and the crew of the *Vital Spark*, Munro was also a successful journalist and historical novelist. He left his native Inverary for Glasgow aged eighteen, working his way up to the editorship of the *Glasgow Evening News* in 1918, at the same time building his reputation as a leading author of historical romance, most notably with *The New Road* (1914). He reported on the war, visiting the front four times. His son Hugh was killed at the Battle of Loos in 1915.

Charles Murray (1864–1941)
From the Aberdeenshire town of Alford, Murray emigrated to South Africa to work as a mining engineer. He served in the Second Boer War with the Railway Pioneer Regiment and as a lieutenant-colonel in the South African Defence Force during the First World War. He returned to Scotland on his retirement in 1924, settling in Banchory.

Murchadh Moireach, Murdo Murray (1890–1964)
A Lewis man, like his close friend John Munro, Murray enlisted in 1914 in the ranks of the 4th Seaforth Highlanders following his graduation from Aberdeen University. He served throughout the war, taking part in the Battles of Neuve Chapelle and the Second Battle of Ypres, and received a commission in 1915. He suffered a serious wound in the arm in 1918. His war diary was published along with a selection of poems in Alasdair I. MacAsgaill (ed.), *Luach na Saorsa* (1970).

Alexander Robertson (1882–1916)
Born in Edinburgh and educated at George Watson's College and Edinburgh University, Robertson completed a BLitt at Oxford University before becoming a lecturer in history at Sheffield University. He enlisted as a private in the 12th York and Lancasters at the outbreak of the First

World War, serving in Egypt and then France. He was killed at Serre on the first day of the Battle of the Somme.

J. B. Salmond (1891–1958)

From Arbroath, where his father was the editor of the *Arbroath Herald*, James Bell Salmond enlisted as a second lieutenant in the 7th Black Watch in 1915, and was promoted to lieutenant in 1917. He was a patient at Craiglockhart Hospital late in 1917 and followed Wilfred Owen as editor of its magazine, *Hydra*. After the war Salmond became editor of the *Scots Magazine* and, later, Head of Manuscripts at St Andrews University Library.

Myra Schneider (1936–)

Born in London, Schneider was brought up and went to school in Gourock on the Firth of Clyde. She 'thought of myself as Scottish until well into my teens', but went to university in London where she trained and worked as a teacher. She writes poetry, does poetry workshops, has published three novels for children and teenagers and a memoir of her struggle with cancer.

Alexander Scott (1920–1989)

Born and educated in Aberdeen, Scott's university studies were interrupted by the war when he enlisted in the Royal Artillery, before transferring to the 51st Highland Division of the Gordon Highlanders, then training for the European invasion after their campaign in the desert. Scott landed in Normandy and saw action in the Ardennes and crossing the Rhine, being awarded the MC in 1945. He completed his degree after the war and went on to become a poet and anthologist and the first head of the department of Scottish Literature at the University of Glasgow.

Charles Scott-Moncrieff (1889–1930)

Renowned after the First World War as the translator of Proust's *À la recherche du temps perdu* (as *Remembrance of Things Past*, 1922–1930), C. K. Scott-Moncrieff was born in Stirlingshire and educated at Winchester College and Edinburgh University. Commissioned in the King's Own Scottish Borderers in August 1914, he served continuously with the regiment until 1917 when he was invalided

home after being seriously wounded during the Battle of
Arras.

Duncan Shaw (dates unknown)
We have not been able to trace this Scots writer. The poem
'Pictures', from his 1945 collection *Tristesse and Other Poems*,
refers to the aftermath of Dunkirk.

Sydney Goodsir Smith (1915–1975)
Smith was born to a Scottish mother in New Zealand, until
the family moved to Edinburgh when he was thirteen where
he continued his education before going to Oxford. When
war broke out his asthma made him unsuitable for army
service, so he worked for the War Office teaching English
to the Polish army in Scotland. He adopted and mastered
Scots as his chosen medium and his first collections of poetry
appeared in the 1940s. After the war he became a familiar
figure in Edinburgh literary circles (the 'Rose Street poets')
making friends with Sorley MacLean, Hugh MacDiarmid,
Norman MacCaig, Robert Garioch and others.

Charles Hamilton Sorley (1895–1915)
Born in Aberdeen, the son of the university's professor of
Moral Philosophy, Sorley was educated at Marlborough
College and the University of Jena. He set aside a place at
University College, Oxford in order to enlist at the out-
break of the First World War. A lieutenant in the Suffolk
Regiment, he was promoted to captain in 1915 aged twenty.
He was killed by a sniper at Hulluch during the Battle of
Loos.

Louise Findlay Stewart (dates unknown)
Stewart's poem appeared in her first and only collection,
War Poems Sea and Sky, published in 1948.

Mary Symon (1863–1938)
From a small-landowning family of Pittyvaich in Dufftown,
Symon was educated in Edinburgh and at St Andrews
University. She remained most of her life in Dufftown, and
lectured and wrote on Banffshire dialects, people, and cus-
toms and was a contributor to the *Scots Magazine* and Hugh
MacDiarmid's *Northern Numbers*.

William J. Tait (1918–1992)

Born on Yell in the Shetlands, Tait was educated and trained as a teacher in Edinburgh. He taught in Lerwick and served in the Home Guard during the war. He was a founder member and contributor to the journal *The New Shetlander* after the war, and his use of Shetland dialect in some of his poems and translations was influential. He became a regular in Edinburgh poetry circles during the 1960s, before eventually retiring to Shetland. His poems were collected as *A Day Between Weathers* in 1980.

Ruthven Todd (1914–1978)

Born and educated in Edinburgh, Todd studied art and worked as an architect and then a farm labourer before turning to journalism and advertising. In London in the 1930s he moved in the same Fitzrovian literary circles as Geoffrey Grigson, Dylan Thomas and Wyndham Lewis, and started to write poetry and fiction. He was a conscientious objector during the war and moved to America in 1947, and then Mallorca, living as a freelance writer and occasional visiting professor.

Sydney Tremayne (1912–1986)

Born and educated in Ayrshire, Tremayne worked as a cub reporter in Yorkshire and then—for much of the rest of his career—as a journalist and sub-editor for the *Daily Mirror* in London. He was in the Fire Service during the war, and lived a busy professional life, but his poetry is marked by a gentle and observational appreciation of the natural world.

Douglas Young (1913–1973)

Born in Fife, Young studied Classics at St Andrews University and New College, Oxford and was appointed lecturer in Greek at Aberdeen University in 1938. A committed Scottish nationalist he was leader of the SNP from 1942 to 1945. During this time he refused to acknowledge the Westminster government's right to conscript him and duly served a term in Saughton prison. During this time he supported the publication of Sorley MacLean's *Dain do Eimhir* and produced his own first collection, *Auntran Blads* (1943). After the war he continued to work as a Classical scholar and academic at St Andrews and then at the University of North Carolina.

Acknowledgements

The Association for Scottish Literary Studies gratefully acknowledges the help provided and the permissions granted by the following people and publishers. Apologies are offered to those copyright holders who could not be traced, and they are encouraged to get in touch with us.

Marion Angus, *The Lilt: and other verses* (Aberdeen: D. Wyllie & Sons, 1922), with special thanks to Alan J. Byatt.

J. K. Annand, *Selected Poems 1925–1990* (Edinburgh: James Thin, The Mercat Press, 1992), with special thanks to Christine Robinson and Scottish Language Dictionaries.

Archibald Allan Bowman, *Sonnets from a Prison Camp* (London: John Lane, 1919).

Edward Boyd, *Night Flight*, Modern Scots Poets (Glasgow: Scoop Books Ltd., 1945), with special thanks to Cathie Thomson.

John Buchan, *Poems, Scots and English* (London & Edinburgh: T. C. & E. C. Jack, 1917).

Norman Cameron, *Norman Cameron: Collected Poems and Selected Translations*, ed. by Warren Hope and Jonathan Barker (London: Anvil Press Poetry, 1990; new edition, 2011).

William Cameron (Motherwell), *Forward*, 15 August 1914.

R. W. Campbell, *The Making of Micky McGhee: And Other Stories in Verse* (London: George Allen & Unwin, 1916).

W. D. Cocker, *The Dreamer: and other poems* (London and Glasgow: Gowans & Gray, 1920).

G. S. Fraser, *Poems of G. S. Fraser*, ed. by Ian Fletcher and John Lucas (Leicester: Leicester University Press, 1981), with special thanks to Helen Fraser.

Olive Fraser, *The Wrong Music. The Poems of Olive Fraser 1909–1977*, ed. by Helena Shire (Edinburgh: Canongate, 1989), with special thanks to Dr Alisoun Gardner-Medwin.

Robert Garioch, 'During a Music Festival'; 'Property'; 'Letter from Italy' from *Robert Garioch, Collected Poems*, ed. by Robin Fulton (Edinburgh: Polygon, 2004), are reproduced by permission of Polygon, an imprint of Birlinn Ltd. **www.birlinn.com**

Flora Garry, *Collected Poems* (Edinburgh: Gordon Wright Publishing, 1995), with thanks to Steve Savage Publishers.

Jack Gillespie, *Poetic Journal of a Cameron Highlander. Poems written by a soldier during the Second World War* (Studley: History Into Print, 2009), with special thanks to James and Hazel Gillespie.

George Campbell Hay, *Collected Poems and Songs of George Campbell Hay*, ed. by Michel Byrne, vol. 1 (Edinburgh: Edinburgh University Press, 2000), with special thanks to the Lorimer Trust.

John MacDougall Hay, *Their Dead Sons* (London: Erskine MacDonald, 1918).

Hamish Henderson, *Collected Poems and Songs* (Edinburgh: Curly Snake Publishing, 2000), with special thanks to Felicity and Janet Henderson.

J. F. Hendry, *The Bombed Happiness* (London: Routledge, 1942), with special thanks to Robert R. Calder.

Michael Hinton 'The Traveller', in *Scottish Student Verse 1937–1947*, intro. Eric Linklater, The Scottish Union of Students, (Edinburgh: The Ettrick Press, ?1947).

Violet Jacob, *More Songs of Angus, and Others* (London: Country Life and George Newnes, 1918), with special thanks to Malcolm Hutton.

Roderick Watson Kerr, *War Daubs: Poems* (London: John Lane, 1919).

Joseph Lee, *Ballads of Battle* (London: John Murray, 1916); *Work-A-Day Warriors* (London: John Murray, 1917).

Maurice Lindsay, *Collected Poems 1940–1990* (Aberdeen: Aberdeen University Press, 1990), with special thanks to Kirsteen Stokes.

Walter Lyon, *Easter at Ypres 1915, And Other Poems* (Glasgow: James Maclehose & Sons, 1916).

MacKenzie MacBride, *For Those We Love at Home!: and other war songs and ballads* (London: Newberry & Pickering, 1916).

Hugh MacDiarmid, *The Complete Poems of Hugh MacDiarmid*, ed. by Michael Grieve and W. R. Aitken (Manchester: Carcanet, 1993), with permission of Carcanet.

Donald MacDonald, taken from *An Tuil: Anthology of 20th Century Scottish Gaelic Verse*, ed. by Ronald Black (Edinburgh: Polygon, 1999), with permission of Polygon. Translated by Ronald Black.

Patrick MacGill, *Soldier Songs* (London: Jenkins, 1917).

Pittendrigh MacGillivray, *Bog-Myrtle and Peat Reek: verse mainly in the North and South country dialects of Scotland* (Edinburgh: printed privately by the author, 1922).

E. A. Mackintosh, *A Highland Regiment* (London & New York: John Lane, 1917); *War, the Liberator and Other Pieces* (London & New York: John Lane, 1918).

Sorley MacLean, *From Wood to Ridge. Collected Poems in Gaelic and English* (Manchester: Carcanet Press Ltd, 1989), with permission of Carcanet.

Colin McIntyre, taken from *From Oasis into Italy. War Poems and Diaries from Africa and Italy 1940–46*, ed. by Victor Selwyn, Dan Davin, Erik de Mauny, Ian Fletcher (London: Shepheard-Walwyn Ltd., 1983), with special thanks to Mrs Field McIntyre.

Malcolm MacLeod, taken from *The Voice of War. Poems of the Second World War*, ed. by Victor Selwyn, (London: Penguin Books, 1996).

Hamish Mann, *A Subaltern's Musings* (London: John Long, 1918).

Naomi Mitchison, *The Cleansing of the Knife and Other Poems* (Edinburgh: Canongate, 1978); *A Girl Must Live, Stories and Poems* (Glasgow: Richard Drew Publishing, 1990), with permission of David Higham Associates.

Charles Scott-Moncrieff, taken from *The Muse in Arms*, ed. by E. B. Osborn (London: John Murray, 1917).

William Montgomerie, *From Time to Time, Selected Poems* (Edinburgh: Canongate, 1985), with special thanks to Dian Elvin.

Edwin Morgan, *Collected Poems* (Manchester: Carcanet Press Ltd., 1990), with permission of Carcanet.

Edwin Muir, *The Collected Poems of Edwin Muir*, (London: Faber and Faber, 2003), with permission of Faber and Faber.

John Munro, taken from *An Tuil: Anthology of 20th Century Scottish Gaelic Verse*, ed. by Ronald Black (Edinburgh: Polygon, 1999), with permission of Polygon. Translated by Ronald Black.

Neil Munro, *The Poetry of Neil Munro* (Edinburgh: W. Blackwood & Sons, 1931).

Charles Murray, *A Sough o' War* (London: Constable & Co., 1917).

Murdo Murray, taken from *An Tuil: Anthology of 20th Century Scottish Gaelic Verse*, ed. by Ronald Black (Edinburgh: Polygon, 1999), with permission of Polygon. Translated by Ronald Black.

Alexander Robertson, *Comrades* (London: Elkin Mathews, 1916); *Last Poems of Alexander Robertson* (London: Elkin Mathews, 1918).

J. B. Salmond, *The Old Stalker: and other verses* (Edinburgh: The Moray Press, 1936).

Myra Schneider, *Insisting on Yellow: New and Selected Poems* (London: Enitharmon Press, 2000), with special thanks to Myra Schneider.

Alexander Scott, *The Collected Poems of Alexander Scott*, ed. by David S. Robb (Edinburgh: Mercat Press, 1994), with special thanks to Crombie Scott.

Duncan Shaw, *Tristesse and Other Poems* (London: Everybody's Books, 1945).

Sydney Goodsir Smith, *Collected Poems 1941–1975* (London: John Calder, 1975), with special thanks to John Calder and Alma Books.

Charles Hamilton Sorley, *Marlborough and other poems* (London: Cambridge University Press, 1916)

Louise Findlay Stewart, *War Poems Sea and Sky* (Glasgow: McKenzie, Vincent & Co. Ltd, 1948).

Mary Symon, *Deveron Days* (Aberdeen: D. Wylie & Son, 1933).

William J. Tait, *A Day Between Weathers: Collected Poems 1938–1978*. (Edinburgh; Paul Harris Publishing, 1980), with special thanks to Brian Tait.

Ruthven Todd, *The Acreage of the Heart*, Poetry Scotland Series (Glasgow: William McLellan & Co. Ltd., 1944), with permission of David Higham Associates.

Sydney D. Tremayne, *For Whom There Is No Spring* (London: Pendulum Publications, 1946), with special thanks to Sydney Tremaine.

Douglas Young, *Auntran Blads* (Glasgow: William McLellan & Co. Ltd, 1943); *A Braird o Thistles* (Glasgow: William McLellan & Co. Ltd, 1947), with special thanks to Clara Young.